RIT PRESS

Superheroes in Crisis

RIT PRESS

Superheroes in Crisis

ADJUSTING TO SOCIAL CHANGE IN THE 1960s AND 1970s

Jeffrey K. Johnson

Superheroes in Crisis
Adjusting to Social Change in the 1960s and 1970s

RIT Press
90 Lomb Memorial Drive
Rochester, New York 14623-5604
ritpress.rit.edu

Book and cover layout by Lisa Mauro
Printed in the U.S.A.

Cover images

ISBN 978-1-933360-80-5 (PRINT)
ISBN 978-1-933360-81-2 (E-BOOK)

Library of Congress Cataloging-in-Publication Data

Johnson, Jeffrey K., 1972 –
Superheroes in crisis : adjusting to social change in the 1960s and 1970s / Jeffrey K. Johnson, Ph.D.
pages cm.–(Comics studies monograph series)
Includes bibliographical references and index.
ISBN 978-1-933360-80-5 – ISBN 978-1-933360-81-2 (e-book)
1. Comic books, strips, etc.–United States–History and criticism.
2. Superman (Fictitious character) 3. Batman (Fictitious character)
4. Superheroes in literature. 5. Social change in literature
6. Literature and society–United States. I. Title.
PN6725.J643 2013
741.5'352--dc23

2013046603

To Monika: I love you.

Comics Studies Monograph Series
Gary Hoppenstand, Series Editor

Narrative Structure in Comics
Making Sense of Fragments
BARBARA POSTEMA

Superheroes in Crisis
Adjusting to Social Change in the 1960s and 1970s
JEFFREY K. JOHNSON

CONTENTS

COMICS AND STORYTELLING

FOREWORD

Comics and Storytelling

The human condition is one that seems to insist on the need to invent stories. In ancient times, oral storytelling explained the powers of nature and the origins of self. Stories soothed, frightened, and inspired people, but perhaps most importantly, they entertained. With the advent of the industrial revolution and the type of technology that led to the creation of the steamroller printing press, oral storytelling transformed into a printed product, a commodity that could be manufactured at little cost and sold for profit. Large centers of urban populations generated by the industrial revolution's working class subsequently provided a ready audience for such 19th century storytelling forms as the story paper, the penny dreadful, and the dime novel.

As the 19th century came to a close, the process of storytelling discovered a new and powerfully compelling outlet: illustration. Popular hardcover books that were printed at that time often featured lavish interior illustrations, and the most successful fiction magazines in America and Great Britain highlighted eye-catching pictures drawn by the best professional artists. When the pulp magazines replaced dime novels as the most popular form of print storytelling in the early decades of the 20th century, illustration was taken to new heights (or depths, depending on your point of view) with the production of pulp magazines featuring garish color covers that highlighted a wide assortment of pulpwood formulas, from westerns, to hard-boiled detective fiction, to science fiction, and beyond. By the start of the Great Depression in America, the time was right for the transformation of the pulp fiction narratives into a new medium–the comic book–that inverted the relationship of print to pictures, so that language of storytelling had become principally visual.

Newspapers of the 19th century had also recognized the value of illustration in the telling of their stories. Cartoons became particularly effective in lampooning politics and politicians. Single-page cartoons evolved into strips where the illusion of movement and time greatly enhanced the telling of stories, and when color printing was added to the process, the comic strip came to dominate most other forms of entertainment in America during the 1920s and 1930s, rivaling in popularity that other quintessentially visual story form: the movies. By the 1970s, comics discovered yet a new means of production, commodity, and entertainment. The graphic novel elevated what had been previously considered by many a juvenile expression of storytelling into something that was adult and earnest in intent, and it brought the comics medium into community libraries, national bookstore chains, and the university classroom. Today, the graphic novel is discussed in the same breath as "serious" literature, and it is analyzed with similar methodical tools.

Without a doubt, comics have engaged us, amazed us, and entertained us. They rank with the most important expressions of visual storytelling in the 20th century, including film and television, and they continue to inspire new generations of readers and fans.

The RIT Press is pleased to present a monograph series that will offer thoughtful and engaging studies of the graphic novel, comic strip, and comic book. This Comics Monograph series will present the work of the finest scholars in the field of comics studies. These authors will examine the theory and practice of comics storytelling, with graphically noteworthy illustrations provided in each monograph. We hope that you enjoy these delightful books. They will enhance your understanding of one of the most significant methods of visual storytelling in our culture.

Gary Hoppenstand, Ph.D.
Series Editor

ACKNOWLEDGMENTS

While writing is primarily a solitary activity, this book would not exist without the help, guidance, and kindness of numerous individuals. My friends, family, and colleagues provided a firm foundation from which I was able to construct this monograph. I am truly indebted to each of them and feel fortunate that such an extraordinary group of people surrounds me. I offer heartfelt thanks to each of you.

I once again owe Dr. Gary Hoppenstand an extraordinary debt of gratitude that I will undoubtedly never be able to repay. Gary has been my mentor since my first days as a graduate student at Michigan State University, and I have benefitted from his wisdom, advice, and friendship in ways that I can never explain. As with most of my work, I would not have completed this book without Gary's help and encouragement. Thank you as always, Gary.

A special thank you to Nicole Rhoton, Donna Knaff, Gregory Kupsky, Derek Mallett, Christopher McDermott, Jean Nakagawa, and Joshua Fennell, who have supported and encouraged me. Thank you also to Malcolm Magee, Jesse Draper, Ana Holguin, Joe Chambers, Elizabeth Chambers, Mary Marasovich, Heather Keyes, and Jennifer Wistrand for all of your kind words and inspiration.

Molly Cort, my editor at RIT Press: thank you for your patience, thoughtfulness, and positive reinforcement. It cannot be easy to deal with writers' egos and mistakes but you were a joy to work with and I am happy that I had the opportunity to produce this book with your guidance. Special thanks to copy editor John O'Toole, designer Lisa Mauro and Bruce Austin, RIT Press Director.

Thank you, Ted and Toni at Gecko Books and Comics in Kaimuki, HI. They were invaluable in helping me research this book and talking about comic book history in general. If the reader is ever in Honolulu be sure to stop by this shop.

Thank you mom and dad for everything.

And a special thank you to my wife Monika. I deeply appreciate all of your love and support, and I would not have been able to write this book without you. I promise that I will not talk about Superman and Batman as much anymore, although I reserve the right to change my mind regarding this matter.

SUPERHEROES IN CRISIS

INTRODUCTION

In April 2011, the Internet was atwitter with reports that an important American had seemingly turned against his country. A U.S. leader and icon had decided to renounce his American citizenship, and this action had confused and angered a large number of U.S. citizens from across the political spectrum. How could a hero who had once upheld the nation's values now reject his long-held place within the country? *Fox News*, *The New York Times*, and many other news sources reported on the seemingly troublesome event, and numerous Americans expressed shame and dismay. While many interested parties offered their opinions, few of these people had actually read *Action Comics* #900, which contains a short story in which Superman declares that he plans to become a citizen of the entire world instead of only the United States. Yes, a plethora of news agencies reported and a substantial number of Americans were concerned that a fictional comic book superhero had renounced his make-believe U.S. citizenship. While this reaction may at first seem odd or even troubling, it is, in fact, an indicator of Superman's importance to American society and culture. Soon after his first appearance in 1938, the Man of Steel quickly became an American icon and a part of the nation's mythology. DC Comics co-publishers, Jim Lee and Dan DiDio, commented on the story, "Superman is a visitor from a distant planet who has long embraced American values. As a character and an icon, he embodies the best of the American Way. In a short story in *Action Comics* #900, Superman announces his intention to put a global focus on his never-ending battle, but he remains, as always, committed to his adopted home and his roots as a Kansas farm boy from Smallville." In other words, as Superman was adapting to meet a new era's ever-changing expectations, Lee and DiDio were reassuring the American public that the Man of Steel was remaining at his core the same. This book is a study of how Superman and Batman, two comic book icons and legends, attempted to adapt to the changing social and cultural landscapes of the 1960s and 1970s, while also endeavoring to stay essentially the same. Even though this desire to simultaneously both evolve and remain unchanged may sound like a fool's errand, it often accurately highlights and mirrors transformations within many citizens' lives and American society as a whole. Superman and Batman are not only symbols of our collective mythologies, but also cultural barometers that gauge changes within our individual lives and the entirety of our society.

The Dynamic Duo

Since their respective introductions in 1938 and 1939, Superman and Batman have fought both numerous villains and would-be world-conquering madmen. These often colorful foes have provided action and adventure while also creating a binary narrative of good and evil. What most people do not consider is that the two superheroes have also fought against a constant onslaught of cultural pressures and societal changes. The superpair began their careers as 1930s avengers, became patriotic icons during World War II, and after the conflict ended, quickly transformed into postwar company men and fathers. The heroes mirrored the changes that took place in many Americans' lives, and displayed the acceptable social attitudes and understandings to which numerous citizens subscribed. Although Superman and Batman started as crusaders who often fought against symbols of authority, they themselves soon became symbols of the state that encouraged their readers to adhere to social and cultural norms. This conservative outlook left the Man of Steel and the Dark Knight in a predicament during the 1960s revolutionary cultural change and in the decade that followed. Like many Americans, the comic book superheroes had to understand which of the new 1960s social values they should embrace and which they should ignore as passing fads. The two had to adapt to a new era, to change, but how and to what degree this change should happen was unclear—and was not going to be easy. Millions of Americans who were in a similar situation certainly could sympathize with the two superheroes' plight.

The Stories We Tell Our Children

A society can understand much about itself by examining the stories that were created for its children. These tales are often simplified versions of how we perceive the world and in this way say more about ourselves than we often intend to. Our stories frequently capture our hopes, dreams, and fears, and hold a mirror to our faces, even when we pretend not to see ourselves. Fairy tales, adventure stories, and even comic book narratives allow parents and other members of society to explain numerous things about their lives in exciting, fun, and generally nonthreatening ways. Until recently, academics have not studied such narratives often because of a misplaced belief that these sources were of no value. For decades many viewed comic books as "low-culture" or "mass-culture" texts that deserved little notice. This began to change during the late 1970s and early 1980s when a growing number of popular-culture scholars began to stress the importance of film, television, and even comic book narratives. Scholars like Ray Browne and Russel Nye endeavored to expand academic and cognitive horizons, and tirelessly worked to create a better understanding of the popular- and mass-culture narratives that often go mostly unnoticed but reflect and shape our lives in a myriad of ways. This book follows in that honorable tradition and examines how the comic book characters Superman and Batman attempted to adapt to new social orders and understandings during the 1960s and 1970s. Although the two superheroes had often been revised and altered during their early fictional careers, these 1960s and 1970s modifications were arguably the more comprehensive changes since their genesis during the Great Depression. The heroes had to reflect American society's new needs while also remaining true to both their and the nation's core elements. Change too little and the heroes would become antiquated; change too much or in the wrong way and the supermen would become unrecognizable.

Besides the aforementioned Russel Nye and Ray Browne, I would also like to acknowledge John Cawelti and John Fiske's academic research and writing regarding the serious study of film and television. All scholars that focus on popular culture narratives owe Drs. Nye, Browne, Cawelti, and Fiske a huge debt, because much of our work is built on the base that they provided. My understanding of comic book narratives is grounded in these scholars' work, and although I have come to my own theories and interpretations that often differ from these writers, it should be noted I view myself as the latest in this long line of popular-culture scholars. One proto-popular-culture academic who does not receive enough mention for his early work involving mass-culture narratives, and who is a major influence on this study, is John Kouwenhoven. His monograph *Made in America: The Arts in Modern Civilization*, although published in 1948, is strikingly contemporary in argument, style, and tone, and makes the contention that American vernacular art is fundamentally different from its European counterpart and should be judged on its own merits. Kouwenhoven asserts that American art is often more technologically centered, democratic, and functional than more cultivated art forms. He refutes that long-held notion that simple and practical means lesser and that art should be individualist and decorative. Although Kouwenhoven never wrote about comic books, his work and mine share the simple and yet profound understanding that American popular culture is a narrative art form that deserves to be studied because it reveals fundamental truths about who we were and who we are, and often in ways that other texts cannot. At heart this book is a study of America and its culture using comic book superheroes as a window onto parts of our society and ourselves into which we often do not gaze.

Secret Origin Narratives

This book will focus on Superman and Batman's changing identities by examining the comic book narratives that create the heroes' ever-adapting worlds and mythologies. Until recently, comic book stories were generally created to be read as monthly periodicals that could be quickly disposed of and thus not be expected to provide an intentional long-form narrative. Furthermore, because comic book publishers during the 1940s and 1950s assumed that readers would outgrow superhero stories within a few years, most tales were designed to be easily accessible for new readers. In order to be consistently inviting to a fresh audience, important background elements and foundational concepts were continually re-explained and often modernized. New story points were constantly being introduced as old components were disposed of and generally forgotten. Ironically, comic books' throwaway nature and their simple ever-adapting stories created one of the most comprehensive ongoing narratives in human history. While these stories were designed to be rapidly read and disregarded, they have collectively become an American mythology that spans over seventy years and tens of thousands of individual tales. By examining this narrative as a whole, the modern reader is able to better understand social and cultural changes within American society. The comic book's perceived status as a combination of juvenile and "trash" literature allows the researcher to investigate narratives that were produced to be transitory and "unimportant." These narratives are extremely significant because they were often simplistic contemporary understandings that contained little or no pretense, and generally claim to have virtually no artistic, political, or social agendas. This lack of a perceived agenda provides an interesting outlet for investigating social and cultural constructs in places in which few were originally intended. Paradoxically, comic book narratives reveal so much about social and cultural changes because they were designed never to address such weighty issues. Superhero stories were meant to entertain children in cheap monthly doses and little was expected of them.

This monograph is split into four parts, each of which discusses Batman's and Superman's changes during a given period. The first chapter examines the characters' backgrounds and provides a basis for understanding the dramatic transformations that were to come. The three remaining chapters investigate how the heroes adjust to a changing society while continuing to assert their own identities. The book's four chapters are:

Chapter 1 - The Early Years

This chapter focuses on the creation of and changes to Superman's and Batman's narratives from 1938 to 1959. Both of these heroes were created in the late 1930s in attempts to offer outlets for young readers trapped in the Great Depression's miseries. The original Man of Steel and the Dark Knight were rough-and-tumble social avengers who meted out violent vigilante justice in order to punish the types of evildoers that American society in the real world could not stop. These first superheroes were violent champions for a hardened people that demanded they act in such a way. The original versions of Superman and Batman did not conform to the rules against killing, maiming, battling authority figures and law enforcement, or disparaging the U.S. government. Rather, the heroes used their own methods and worked outside the law in a manner of which their readers and many within American society approved. As the nation changed, the superpair also needed to shift their identities. After the U.S.'s entry into World War II, Superman's and Batman's outlooks and natures drastically changed. During this period the two superheroes transformed from social avengers to patriotic war heroes and eventually to conservative family and company men after the conflict's end. During the war, the superpair changed into strong nationalists who obeyed all governmental and military mandates, and worked hard to help the war effort. After combat ended, the two followed numerous cultural and social examples and transitioned into new lives as pseudo-fathers and protectors of the state. Many Americans desired a calm and peaceful postwar society and Superman and Batman endeavored to protect the new norm, not to change it. The heroes' new outlooks reflected characters that were in touch with the conventional values of the era, along with an understanding of the nation's mood and outlook.

Chapter 2 - Middle-Age Changes

This chapter explores how Superman and Batman narratives changed from 1960 to 1969 in order to deal with social and cultural upheavals. As younger fans began to flock to more counterculture-friendly Marvel superheroes, the Man of Steel and the Dark Knight faced the 1960s in very different ways. While both heroes began the decade as trustworthy and gray quasi-superfathers and pseudo-company men, Batman soon transformed into a cerebral detective who differed greatly from his often strange 1950s self. The Caped Crusader quickly altered himself again, though, and by the mid-1960s his comic book modeled the camp features of the *Batman* television series. Much like the television show, this version of Batman did not last long and by decade's end the Dark Knight had a new dark and moody focus. While Batman radically changed several times during the ten-year period, Superman attempted to make only minor adjustments without committing to major changes. The Man of Steel essentially remained a conservative 1950s icon, even as the world around him drastically shifted.

Chapter 3 - The Early 1970s — Self-Doubt and Worry

This chapter centers on how Superman and Batman, much like the country around them, intently struggled to adjust to a post-1960s world. During the early 1970s, many Americans started to question the previous decade's changes and a large number of citizens wondered if American society had ventured too far from its traditional foundation. As many people were trying to understand and refashion the 1960s' social modifications, Superman and Batman writers and artists were also looking to comprehend how the two superheroes should act in the modern world. For a time, the author Denny O'Neil wrote both characters and tried to modernize them by making them more serious and less powerful. Although these changes did not last long, they do show the superheroic duo's struggles to remain viable in an ever-changing world.

Chapter 4 - Where Do We Go From Here? 1975 – 1979

This chapter emphasizes how Superman and Batman's creative teams dealt with the mood and tone of American society in the mid- to late 1970s. From 1975 to 1979, the United States suffered numerous problems and setbacks, and many Americans began to question the nation's direction and future. Watergate, the Vietnam War, an energy crisis, and an economic downturn pushed the nation into a period of social stagnation. During this time, Superman and Batman stories reflected the growing malaise and showcased superheroes who, like their society, had lost their way. Superman remained an overly powerful traditional 1950s-style character who had attempted to change numerous times but was unable to complete a lasting transition. The once-proud Man of Steel now relied on over-used gimmicks and out-of-date story ideas that made him appear to be a shell of his former self. Batman also battled the mid- and late-1970s malaise but, as in times past, was much more willing to adjust to a new social and cultural environment. The Dark Knight fought crooked politicians and urban criminals as Americans increasingly worried about such things. Batman also worked hard to remain vibrant and fresh even as the country was facing a period of stagnation. As they did in every other period, the two heroes tried to adapt to the changing times in far different ways.

Notes

1 Holly McKay. "Superman Renounces His U.S. Citizenship in 900th Issue of Action Comics," Foxnews.com. Accessed December 20, 2011. http://www.foxnews.com/entertainment/2011/04/28/superman-renounces-citizenship-900th-issue/.

Fig. 0.1
A group of Great Depression era children in St. Augustine, Texas enjoy a comic book. U.S. Farm Security Administration/Office of War Information, Library of Congress, 1939.

CHAPTER 1

The Early Years: Original Heroes

Both Superman and Batman were created and debuted during the Great Depression, and because of this, the characters' personalities were a reflection of the era's hopes and fears. The two comic book superheroes were designed to grapple with nemeses that threatened common Americans during this tumultuous time, and to provide readers a means of temporary literary escape. Although the heroes were created to battle social and political menaces, World War II caused major changes in the fictional heroes' lives and stories. The two costumed avengers no longer attempted to change American society, but rather seemed to wish only to protect the nation against all threats foreign and domestic. Superman and Batman became super-patriotic Americans and top-notch war-bond salesmen who worried more about citizens' physical safety and less about producing social change. The superduo became protectors of the social and political status quo, a stance that would only grow firmer after the war's end. In the late 1940s and throughout the 1950s the Man of Steel and the Dark Knight would morph into superpowered company men and agents of the state. No longer were they vigilantes who enforced their own code of right and wrong; rather they were clean-cut costumed G-Men who followed the letter of the law and strongly encouraged their readers to do the same. By the start of the 1950s, Superman and Batman had become law enforcement agents who fought to uphold social and cultural norms and did not tolerate actions that deviated from accepted societal standards. Numerous elements and factions of American society had worked together to co-opt the onetime outsiders and transform them into the ultimate representatives of the state. These were only the first of the superpair's many transformations, and the heroes and their creators would soon learn that American society would demand they evolve even more as the years progressed. Americans oxymoronically expected both Superman and Batman, as cultural icons and social mirrors, to forever remain both classic and modern.

Jerry Siegel and Joe Shuster fashioned Superman as a Great Depression social avenger who fought against common criminals like wife-beaters, crooked politicians, and corrupt landlords. Similarly, writer and artist Bob Kane designed Batman to be a hardcore vigilante who battled a vast array of criminals. Both members of this superheroic duo were rough-and-tumble righters-of-wrongs who were reflections of their societies and eras. Superman first appeared in *Action Comics* #1, cover dated June 1938, and was a fictional ray of hope for an America that had been suffering economic, social, and environmental hardships for almost a decade. Millions of Americans were out of work and even more had descended into hopelessness, and Superman served as a bright spot in this bleak and depressing age. In his first storyline, the Man of Steel grapples with a myriad of Great Depression era foes, including crooked politicians, mobsters, and wife-beaters. In these earliest appearances, Superman battles the types of criminals that plagued average American citizens of the era. The Man of Steel acts like an idealistic young man and attempts to solve society's problems in simplistic and often naïve ways. In *Action Comics* #2, the new comic book hero continues to combat a war profiteer whom he had humiliated and scared in the previous issue. Superman physically intimidates the man and forces him to join the military and fight in an unnecessary war that was started to sell an increased amount of munitions. After the Man of Tomorrow gives him a good drubbing, the warmonger repents of his former lifestyle and Superman proves that the threat of physical violence can solve almost any problem. At issue's end, our hero terminates the war by convincing the two armies' leaders that they have nothing to fight about and thus should not fight at all. Superman had ended an armed conflict and changed an unethical businessman's behavior in one short comic book issue.[1] This new superhero was the type of protector that his society demanded and probably needed.

Many early Superman stories follow the same basic outline of the tale in *Action Comics* #1 and #2. The Man of Steel physically intimidates, injures, or even kills those he believes should be punished, and either they change their ways or Superman disposes of them. Often his enemies are not even breaking the law, but rather are violating the new hero's personal moral code. This 1930s version of the Man of Steel displays a young man's recklessness and naivety, and he generally appears to be as much crazed bully as hero. Superman rushes from place to place and engages his foes in a rapid, almost manic, manner. The Man of Tomorrow delights in humiliating and subjugating what he perceives to be society's enemies and seems to relish abusing and often harming "bad guys." The hero's short attention span, his joyful ill-treatment of wrongdoers, and his disregard for any point of view except his own also mark him as a young man probably still in his adolescence. This first version of Superman is a superpowered street brawler who often ignores the law and uses whatever methods he deems necessary to uphold his moral code. He is a young man, created by young men, who innocently believes that he can find simple solutions to the complicated problems that exist within the world. Superman is rough-and-tumble, and abusive, but also is honest, guileless, and unpretentious. He is a plainspoken blue-collar (and red-caped) superhero who identifies with the masses and truly believes society's most powerful members are maltreating ordinary citizens. Superman may be a bully, but he is the common man's bully, and is the only one strong enough to oppose wealthy businessmen, corrupt government officials, and other members of the ruling class. At his inception, the Man of Steel is an ultrapowerful being who fights for his understanding of the common good. He is a version of Superman who believes in and protects the common man.

Superman's early adventures showcase his populist leanings and his aggressive, yet whimsical, nature. One early text box described the costumed hero as "... Superman, savior of the helpless and oppressed, in his never-ceasing war on injustices!"[2] In *Action Comics* #3 the Man of Steel disguises himself as a coal miner and traps the mine owner and his socialite friends underground in order to show them the importance of safety regulations and working men. In future issues, Superman drugs a college football player and steals his identity in order to rig a football game so that professional gamblers cannot manipulate the contest's outcome (*Action Comics* #4); stops a crooked businessman who claims to be the Man of Steel's manager (*Action Comics* #6); saves a destitute circus from bankruptcy and punishes the big top's would-be saboteurs (*Action Comics* #7); crusades for more humane prison conditions (*Action Comics* # 10); battles against stock fraud (*Action Comics* #11); and declares war on reckless drivers (*Action Comics* #12). One of the strangest and most interesting stories appeared in January 1939's *Action Comics* #8 in which Superman befriends a gang of juvenile delinquents who have run afoul of the law. Superman beats up the adult criminal for whom the boys fence stolen goods and eventually throws the grown-up wrongdoer head first into a barrel of tar. The Man of Steel fights two police officers who have apprehended one of the young criminals, and snatches the boy from police custody. Even as Superman is breaking the law to help them, the young lads engage in robbing local houses and violating other laws. Superman believes, "It's not entirely your fault that you're delinquents–it's these slums–your poor living conditions ..."[3] The Man of Tomorrow eventually decides that the best way to help these hooligans, and others like them, is to destroy all of the houses in the economically depressed area where they live. As Superman demolishes the homes of the underprivileged, U.S. military ground forces attempt to shoot the Man of Tomorrow and a squadron of bombers targets him. The Man of Steel does not let the military stop him though, as he continues on his destructive rampage. Soon the urban area is completely obliterated and the government is forced to build new apartment complexes that contain "... splendid housing conditions."[4] In this issue, the Man of Steel sides with young criminals but manhandles older lawbreakers, battles the police, wars with the military, and destroys private property in order to force the U.S. and/or state and local governments to build better public housing. Superman believes himself to be a champion of the everyman and works hard to right what modern readers may often see as minor wrongs. This young and boisterous Man of Steel identifies with liberal causes, which he believes benefit the poor and the overlooked. His social and cultural ideas and understandings are very different from the hero that he would become, and his beliefs are a contrast to the things that Batman fights for during the late 1930s.

Liberal Supermen and Conservative Bats

While the *über*powerful 1930s Superman displays the manners and style associated with common Americans of the era, the Great Depression era Batman economically, socially, and culturally separates himself from the rabble that surrounds him.[5] The Caped Crusader both substantively and stylistically withdraws from the bourgeois social norm. If the Man of Steel is a liberal populist, then the Dark Knight is a conservative elitist. Superman takes on the secret identity of Clark Kent and works at a local newspaper while Batman is Bruce Wayne, a wealthy industrialist who does not labor but instead lives the life of a carefree playboy. Superman is extraordinarily powerful but identifies with the common man; Batman is an ordinary human who has trained himself to be mentally and physical superior to the average human. Superman shows his face for all to see and disguises himself when he is Clark Kent, while Batman dons a mask in order to hide his true identity. Batman chooses to be closed off and sequestered from the very society that he wishes to protect. Although Superman is an alien, he has integrated himself into American society, while Batman has created a barrier between himself and the world around him. The Dark Knight lives in a secluded manor (and manner) and chooses to fight crime at night, so that he can become a symbol of terror to criminals. Alternatively, Superman is a symbol of hope and prefers to battle injustice when most of the populace is awake. Superman represents the New Deal Democrats that backed Franklin Roosevelt's social programs, while Batman personifies the conservative Horatio Alger-like notion of the individual helping himself. Neither of these heroes' first incarnations would last long, but even at the beginning, the two founding fathers of superhero comic books have very different perspectives and styles.

Batman's first stories present the Caped Crusader as a dark, threatening, and mysterious figure who battles exceptional and often world-threatening menaces. The Dark Knight premiered in *Detective*

Comics #27 (cover dated May 1939) and during his first two years he fought evil scientists, crazed werewolf religious leaders, dictators, and numerous other megalomaniacal madmen. Batman's villains were generally more powerful and evil than the everyday corrupt businessmen, politicians and other rule-breakers that Superman routinely warred against. The conservative Dark Knight normally wasted little effort on common criminals but instead habitually elected to take on extreme wrongs. The ultrapowerful Superman did not fight vampires and cult-leading werewolves, and only occasionally battled criminals or villains that could offer any type of resistance. Not weighed down by egalitarian notions, Batman preferred to associate himself with a better class of criminal. The Caped Crusader's first adventure in *Detective Comics* #27 features him investigating murders that stemmed from a business dispute between partners. In the next issue, the Dark Knight apprehends jewel thieves and in the following two stories faces down the villainous researcher Dr. Death. Later tales showcase Batman fighting the aforementioned werewolf/monk, a dirigible-riding Napoleon look-alike would-be world conqueror, a vampire, an explorer/adventurer, a professor, and a foreign agent. Each of these scoundrels plagued society's social and economic upper echelons, and were vastly different from the mostly lower-level criminals that Superman routinely fought. The dark and mysterious Batman warred with academics, wealthy businessmen, and world travelers while creating a terrifying persona designed to scare common criminals. The elitist hero kept high society safe from upper-class criminals as Superman protected the common man from those more powerful than him. The heroes were from the same time and place but represented vastly different Americas.

Superman and Batman seemingly had little in common during the late 1930s, as neither could agree on style, outlook, or the type of criminal they preferred to battle. One thing they did share, though, was their willingness to engage in brutality when fighting wrongdoers. Twenty-first-century superhero fans generally think of Superman and Batman as costumed avengers that supplement law enforcement's efforts to uphold the law. The heroes' current versions frequently physically fight criminals and Batman often beats up evildoers, but both would be loath to kill or maim a lawbreaker. This code against killing did not exist for either of the two heroes during their early months. Superman often harmed and sometimes seemingly killed wrongdoers, and Batman caused the deaths of many bad guys and showed little remorse. Examples abound, as in the Dark Knight's introductory tale in which he punches a law-breaking industrialist, forcing the evildoer to fall into a vat of acid and causing Batman to exclaim, "A fitting ending for his kind."[6] In March 1940's *Detective Comics* # 37, Batman pushes a malicious count onto a well-placed sword, to which the Dark Knight opines, "Dead! It is better that he should die!..."[7] Superman rarely explicitly kills criminals, but often he severely harms then and sometimes puts them in situations that lead to their deaths. In *Action Comics* #1 Superman roughs up several citizens and an elected government official. The Man of Steel tortures a prison superintendent in *Action Comics* #10, force-feeding the official prisoners' meals and making the terrified man endure the hot and suffocating conditions of the sweatbox. In *Action Comics* #13, Superman accidently drops a criminal from a great height, resulting in the man's death. Superman shows no remorse but instead moralizes, ". . . the fate he received was exactly what he deserved."[8] Possibly most disturbingly, in *Superman* #5, The Man of Steel seemingly purposely electrocutes a criminal.[9] Both Batman and Superman acted like reckless and aggressive adolescents during their early adventures. The two heroes threatened, tortured, and sometimes even killed, but this would all soon change. A number of social and political events would transform the heroes' lives and would force the costumed pair to grow up.

And Robin Makes Two

Superman and Batman began their comic book adventures as aggressive young men who worked outside the law to bring a personal type of justice to American society. Superman aimed to help the common man while Batman policed the upper class. Like most Great Depression young men, the two heroes had to grow up quickly and rapidly change their ways. Superman's and Batman's youthful period lasted only for a short time before they were forced to take on more responsibility and embrace a newfound attitude. The Caped Crusader's maturation process is the easiest to track and came about in much the same way as many other men's. Like millions of males throughout history, Batman had to mature quickly when he became responsible for a child. In April 1940, *Detective Comics* #38 introduced Robin the Boy Wonder and soon Batman had both a new professional partner and a sonlike figure in his life. This early Robin is nine-year-old Dick Grayson, the son of circus performers who are murdered by gangsters as Bruce Wayne watches from the audience. Batman quickly trains the pre-adolescent Grayson to be a masked avenger and dresses him in a bright and garish red, yellow, and green outfit. Bruce Wayne becomes Dick Grayson's legal guardian and Robin becomes Batman's crime-fighting partner.[10] While the idea of authorizing a nine-year-old boy to wear a costume and battle criminals does not sound very well thought out (and would be considered child abuse by most Americans today), Robin's presence does force Batman to become more stable and mature. True, Bruce Wayne did not adopt Dick Grayson as his son, but the eccentric billionaire was for all intents and purposes a father figure to the young man. Like most fathers, Batman has to adjust his lifestyle in order to meet his new parental responsibilities. Although the Caped Crusader still attempts to frighten and intimidate wrongdoers, his adventures no longer have the same dark and forbidding tone as before. Batman could not easily blend into the shadows and thrash criminals with impunity anymore. Now most of Batman's tales take place in well-lit and brightly colored environs, and the Dark Knight rarely seems to venture out after dusk. (This may be because Dick had to adhere to an early bedtime.) Robin's bright red and yellow costume makes it impossible to sneak stealthily through the night and instead, Batman adjusts to the exuberant young lad. After April 1940, Batman was still the Dark Knight but Robin's introduction lightened him up considerably.

It did not take long for Batman to transform from a dark and brooding justice-obsessed crime fighter into a patient teacher who dotes on his young partner like an approving father. In Robin's second appearance in May 1940's *Detective Comics* #39, Batman smiles widely as he watches the Boy Wonder thrash a pair of villains and notes to himself, "Well, doggone! All I can say is, he certainly is an apt pupil."[11] At the end of the story in *Detective Comics* #42 (July 1940), Robin has broken up a nefarious crime operation at a private boys' school and asks Batman how he performed, to which the Dark Knight replies, "All I've got to say is . . . if you're as terrific, as you are as a kid . . . I pity the criminals when you're a grown man."[12] Oddly, October 1940's *Detective Comics* #44 features a story that is almost entirely one of Robin's fairy-tale-like dreams in which he and Batman visit a land of giants and little people.[13] This bright and colorful tale is very different from Batman's early solo adventures and seems to assert metatextually Robin's newfound importance. While the Caped Crusader was once a solitary menacing vigilante, he now has become an often cheerful father figure who offers smiling praise and shares his life with a nine-year-old boy. Batman still fights crime and continues to stop criminals from breaking the law, but he no longer threatens and terrorizes evildoers. Instead he has changed his ways in order to incorporate a child into his life. Batman is maturing and taking on more responsibility, but can the same be said of Superman?

Don't Go Changing

As Batman was adjusting to his new life as a surrogate father figure, Superman was still enjoying his carefree childless days. The early Man of Steel was known for his playful sense of humor, aggressiveness, and his belief only in his own version of morality and justice, which often differed from legal statutes. By the middle of 1940, the conservative Batman had found himself an heir and was already training the next generation of crime fighters, while Superman was still attempting to remake American society into a young man's liberal fantasy. The Man of Steel's maturation process is much more gradual and harder to notice than Batman's abrupt acceptance of responsibility. Throughout the late 1930s and the early 1940s, Superman continued to battle small-time criminals and fight seemingly minor social problems. During the Man of Tomorrow's first three years he still warred against racketeers, con men, corrupt businessmen, mobsters, and even worked to stop children from spending their money in slot machines.[14] Slowly though, Superman began to take on greater challenges and tackled his supertasks with increasingly constrained brutality and a more serious manner. Although the Man of Steel continued to taunt and physically manhandle villains, he did so with less frequency and vigor. Superman did not make a showy announcement that he was going to curtail his aggressive and sometimes juvenile ways, rather he began to confront challenges with enhanced seriousness and a seemingly greater work ethic. Superman was an incredibly powerful individual who in many ways during his early years stayed a boy at heart. While Batman chose to jump-start the maturation process by raising a surrogate son, Superman slowly and deliberately followed the path towards manhood.

In the first twelve issues of *Action Comics* (June 1938-May 1939) Superman battled no one that could match him physically or mentally. He was a (super)man among boys who physically intimidated weaker wrongdoers. Superman was pure wish fulfillment for American readers who wanted to find someone powerful enough to bully society's bullies. In these initial twelve Superman stories, the Man of Steel physically threatens and intimidates someone twenty-eight times. This is an average of 2.33 times per story. During the Man of Tomorrow's sophomore year in *Action Comics* #13-24 (June 1939 to May 1940), Superman commits approximately sixteen physically threatening acts of intimidation, averaging about 1.33 per story, or about one fewer physical threat per issue than the prior year. During the Man of Steel's third year, in *Action Comics* #25-36 (June 1940 to May 1941), he commits approximately nine intimidating acts or about .75 each story.[15] This is a substantial decline and shows that the Man of Tomorrow committed over two-thirds fewer violent acts in year three than he had just two years before. Superman did not become a pacifist, but he did instigate fewer violent acts and seemed to take less joy in scaring and harming criminals. This gradual methodological change can be seen in *Action Comics* #18, a second-year Superman story. In this tale, the Man of Steel breaks into a blackmailer's apartment and takes away a bow and arrow which the wrongdoer is brandishing. Superman does not punch the man, dangle him out the window, or tuck the lawbreaker under his arm while jumping across power-lines, as he would have in previous adventures. Instead our costumed hero fires an arrow that perfectly hits and destroys a single light bulb on a sign across the street, displaying a skillful use of his powers which the reader has rarely witnessed before.[16] This constrained yet impressive display of his powers appears to scare the criminal as much as past presentations of brute force. Superman seemed to be willing to let the wrongdoer's imagination do the work that the Metropolis Marvel's muscles would have done in the past. As he matured, the Man of Steel began embracing subtlety instead of excessiveness and skillfulness over brute force.

Besides Superman's gradual shift from favoring excessive force to embracing a more restrained existence, one other change helps mark the Man of Steel's slow maturation process. Interestingly, this transition also began in *Action Comics* #13, the start of Superman's second year. In this story, Superman first encounters the evil would-be world-conquering genius known as the Ultra-Humanite. This megalomaniacal madman introduces himself to Superman by stating, "... You may possess unbelievable strength–but you are pitting yourself against a mental giant! . . .A scientific experiment resulted in my possessing the most agile and learned brain on earth! –Unfortunately for mankind, I prefer to use this great intellect for crime. My goal? **Domination of the world!!**" (bold in the original).[17] While the insane bald paraplegic would-be world dictator's characteristics now read like a long list of bad comic book villain traits, the Ultra-Humanite is, in fact, the first supervillain and a reoccurring nemesis that the Man of Steel must repeatedly face. Before meeting this intellectually superior adversary, Superman happily battled only physically and mentally weaker foes. The Man of Steel was content with taking on ordinary criminals who offered little resistance and had no hope of ever defeating him. The Ultra-Humanite is the first antagonist who could possibly best the vaunted Man of Tomorrow. Superman proves vulnerable while fighting this crazed scientist though, and now must increasingly engage in real battles rather than the preachy bullying sessions that had become the norm. The Ultra-Humanite sets a new adversarial standard, and although Superman will continue to fight small-time hoods and provide easy solutions for social ills, he progressively will begin to battle both supervillains and world-shaping problems. The Man of Steel fights the Ultra-Humanite in six different stories from June 1939 through February 1940 until the villain suddenly disappears, not to return for decades. Superman cannot revert to his former less stressful existence though, because in April 1940's *Action Comics*

#23, the Man of Steel first encounters the man who will be his archnemesis, Lex Luthor. Soon Superman is not only fighting more supervillains but also battling natural disasters and diseases, and trying to prevent impending wars. The Man of Steel is no longer content to tackle easily solved problems, but rather works to save the world from greater threats. Superman is taking on more responsibility and is using his amazing powers to solve larger and more substantial problems. While the Man of Steel still continues to battle lower-level threats, world-altering villains and events command an increasing amount of his attention. Superman has not forgotten the common man but he is maturing enough to accept a greater amount of responsibility.

Fig. 0.2 The nose art on this B-17 Flying Fortress displays Superman's popularity among American servicemen during World War II. Margaret Bourke-White/ Time & Life Pictures/ Getty Images

A Nation At War

As Superman and Batman were maturing and accepting more personal and social responsibility, world events were forcing the superduo to adapt even more. In September 1939, Germany invaded Poland and much of the world was quickly plunged into the conflict that would soon become known as World War II. The U.S. would not enter the war until December 1941, but, like the country, many comic book superheroes began preparing to battle the Axis powers long before their nation joined the fray. Superman had flirted with earlier measures against aggressive foreign nations but did not completely commit to the war effort until after the Pearl Harbor bombings. The Man of Steel fought against unscrupulous lobbyists and crooked politicians who wanted to embroil the U.S. in a European war in his first story in *Action Comics* #1 and 2, over a year before World War II began. Superman also stops a civil war in the faux country of Boravia in a story in *Superman* #2, published in the fall of 1939, and ends a European war orchestrated by the evil genius Lex Luthor in *Superman* #9 (March/April 1941), in which the Man of Steel stops saboteurs from harming military production, and *Superman* #10 (May/June 1941), in which he battles fascists and foreign spies. One of the most interesting stories involving Superman and war appeared in the February 27, 1940 issue of *Look Magazine*. In this two-page tale entitled "How Superman Would End the War," the Man of Steel quickly captures Adolf Hitler and Josef Stalin and hands them over to the League of Nations, where the German and Soviet leaders are tried for their crimes.[18] Unfortunately, Superman was unable to end the actual war so quickly, although he and Batman would soon become major proponents of the war effort.

Superman fought against warmongering and unchecked aggression before the U.S. entered World War II, but starting in 1942 the Man of Steel became a full-fledged supporter of the Allies' cause. Although the Man of Steel was gradually evolving by early 1942, during his first two and a half years, Superman was generally portrayed as an anti-authority hero who battled against social ills and often clashed with law enforcement officers. On more than one occasion, the Man of Tomorrow fought the U.S. military and warred against both ground soldiers and aircraft pilots. The U.S. declaration of war quickly changed Superman's attitude, and the Man of Steel became a fervent supporter of the Armed Services and a deeply patriotic citizen. Where Superman had once been a rogue vigilante, now he was in lockstep with the U.S. war effort and was rarely critical of authority figures. The comic book hero had been slowly maturing, but the war quickly changed the Man of Steel into a much different character. A February 16-18, 1942, Superman daily newspaper comic strip story explained that Clark Kent tried to enlist in the military but was unable to pass the eye exam when his x-ray vision malfunctioned and he read the eye chart in the next room. Later in this story Superman states, "The United States Army, Navy and Marines are capable of smashing their foes without the aid of a Superman! Perhaps I could be of more use to my country working right here at home, battling the saboteurs and Fifth Columnists who will undoubtedly attempt to wreck our production of vital war materials."[19] This storyline allowed creators and editors to both present the Man of Steel as a patriotic citizen and explain why he was not serving overseas and winning the war. Superman was protecting American society, much as he always had, but now he was working with the U.S. government and following many generally accepted social norms. Before, Superman had been an untamed force of nature who played by his own rules, now he was just another American hoping that his country would win the war.

As World War II progressed, Superman appeared in a number of stories dedicated to the war effort, many of which celebrated U.S. servicemen and women. One of the most patriotic was a tale from *Superman* #23 (July/August 1943) entitled "America's Secret Weapon." In this story Superman takes part in military war games and his team loses to a group of American servicemen. Throughout the text, the Man of Steel acts extremely patriotic and states things like, "American soldiers cheering me, when all civilized peoples in the world are cheering them! It's the grandest tribute I've ever had!"[20] After losing the war simulation, Superman emphatically states, "I hope the whole world hears of this and of our nation's real secret weapon–the unflagging courage of her men, no matter what the odds, and their indomitable will to win! Against that, Hitler and Hirohito haven't a ghost of a chance." The Man of Steel continues, "And now, it's my turn to cheer! Hooray for the American fighting man–the real champion on land, on the sea and in the air!"[21] In just a few short months, Superman went from an anti-authoritarian vigilante to a literal cheerleader for the military in particular and the country's leadership in general. This transformation is undoubtedly a mixture of governmental pressure to produce war propaganda and the creators' and editors' inherent patriotic sentiments. No matter what the cause, Superman was no longer the New Deal warrior that served only his ideal of justice. After the start of the World War II, the Man of Steel quickly became an agent of the state and submitted to both national and local authority. Like many citizens of the time, Superman was now falling in line and accepting a new role in American society.

Much like Superman, Batman also began fighting against Axis invaders and plotters on the home front. The Dark Knight, along with Robin the Boy Wonder, did his best to keep the United States free of spies and saboteurs. The Dynamic Duo continued to uncover secret plots and nefarious war-related criminal activities throughout the conflict. There are numerous examples of Batman and Robin's war adventures but one of the most emblematic is a *Batman* #14 (December 1942/January 1943) story entitled "Swastika Over the White House!" In this tale, a German spy and saboteur poses as a paparazzo to become a newsreel cameraman, so that he can film footage of American industrial and military secrets. The German secret agent is part of a larger spy ring which has planned acts on sabotage on American soil and eventually wishes to turn the White House into Adolf Hitler's American headquarters. At one point in the story, the main spy muses, "How easy it is to trick people of these trusting democracies!"[22] Eventually Batman and Robin thwart the German scheme and capture the bad guys. (The story culminates with Batman and Robin finding the spy ring's secret headquarters and dropping a large swastika-shaped lighting fixture on the German agents.) Another story, "The Two Futures!" from *Batman* #15 (February/March 1943), has Batman and Robin visiting a local university where three brilliant historians describe two possible futures, one in which the Allies win World War II and one in which they lose. The tale begins with a text box introduction that notes, "Have you wondered what is in store for America–and for you–when the slave armies of the insane dictators have ended their murderous assault upon the decent and peaceful nations of the world?"[23] In the *A Christmas Carol* like narrative, Batman and Robin are transported to a future in which the Axis powers have won the war and have invaded the United States. This bleak and despondent dystopian alternate future America is filled with concentration camps, routine violence against citizens, and horrible living conditions for everyone except German and Japanese military personnel. The Dynamic Duo battle the Axis overlords but are eventually captured and face a firing squad. In contrast, in the second possible future, the two caped crime fighters help the Allies win the war, and the U.S. becomes a peaceful and prosperous country that literally features a shiny golden city on a hill, and young American children who do not have to go to war because ". . . Uncle Sam taught the people of the world a lesson."[24] The story ends with Batman and Robin urging readers to buy war bonds and ration scarce material, so that the second future can become a reality. Much like Superman, Batman is now a cheerleader and pitchman for the war industry, and a great deal of the menacing character that he had once been has now disappeared.

As Superman and Batman were fighting Nazi and Japanese menaces on the home front, the superpair were also becoming supersalesmen. Like many celebrities and popular culture characters, both Superman and Batman joined the effort to change American society during the war. The superduo took part in propaganda campaigns that encouraged Americans to recycle and ration, and the heroes reminded readers to put servicemen first by following all of the new governmental guidelines and rules. One of the most noticeable of Superman's and Batman's war-related activities is their efforts to encourage Americans to buy war bonds as a way to loan the government money to fund war operations. These war bond advertisements were sometimes featured as part of a regular story, as was discussed in the abovementioned tale in *Batman* #15. Besides creating tales to hawk war bonds, creators often fashioned comic book covers that served as minipropaganda posters designed to increase the sale of these debt securities. These covers generally showcased one or more of our heroes fighting against America's enemies, but rarely connected to a story featured inside the magazine. Some examples of these covers are *Action Comics* #59 (April 1943) which shows Superman tearing apart a Nazi tank with a text box that reads, "War Bonds and Stamps Smash Axis Tanks Too!"; *Batman* #15 which depicts Batman firing a machine gun as Robin feeds ammunition into the weapon with the caption "Keep Those Bullets Flying! Keep on Buying War Bonds & Stamps!"; and *Action Comics* #58, in which Superman operates a giant printing press that produces posters which read, "Superman says: YOU Can Slap a Jap With War Bonds and Stamps." By 1942 Superman and Batman had not only become super-war bond salesmen but were happily encouraging Americans to fall in line and follow all of the government's war mandates. Any touch of the anti-authority views that both had formerly held was now gone. Superman and Batman were henceforth safer and more law-abiding versions of their former selves.

As Superman and Batman were becoming superpatriotic nationalistic social pitchmen, their stories also became more mainstream and less radical. The two heroes who had originally been created to be aggressive vigilantes who warred against evildoers and law officials alike. Political and social changes combined to force Superman and Batman to evolve into nicer and safer heroes. By 1942, Superman and Batman stories sometimes included World War II-based plots or Axis-related villains, but most stories feature the superheroes battling ordinary criminals or villains. Superman fights many of the same opponents as he had before, along with numerous more powerful adversaries, while taking special care not to act aggressively or menacingly towards law enforcement. The Metropolis Marvel now not only battles stronger and more intelligent opponents, but also fights silly villains like the Puzzler, Toyman, and the fifth-dimensional imp Mr. Mxyzptlk. The Man of Steel even has to deal with Lois Lane's niece, Susie Tompkins, a precocious young girl whose wild imagination and tall tales consistently create problems for the hero. This is a far cry from the Superman of only a few years before who was terrifying criminals and aggressively warring against social and political wrongs. Like Superman's, Batman and Robin's adventures became brighter and more light-hearted and generally were not nearly as grim and violent as before. The Dynamic Duo still physically battled numerous criminals, but their adventures no longer had the dangerous feeling of the early Dark Knight stories. Instead, Batman is content to clash with comical villains like the Penguin, to help right minor wrongs, and to share his stories with a list of new characters like his butler, Alfred. In one story from this period, Batman and Robin help a young fan who is tricked into committing a series of crimes. At the story's end, the Dynamic Duo enroll the boy in military school and consider their work done. The pair seems happy to have helped the young lad and appears to be less worried about warring against crime than helping the deserving.[25] American society's World War II needs changed Superman and Batman greatly before, during, and after the war years. The heroes who had once battled all wrongdoers, no matter what the perpetrator's identity or legal affiliation, now squarely worked within the system. The Man of Steel and the Dark Knight were no longer outsiders but now full agents of the state. As the U.S. was undergoing many alterations during the war, Batman and Superman were also transforming. Would these changes be temporary or would they remain? At war's end, that question still remained unanswered.

A Secure New World

Superman and Batman became upstanding citizens and intensely patriotic Americans during World War II, but by autumn 1945, the conflict was over and the U.S. was attempting to transition back to a peacetime society. During the previous generation, President Warren G. Harding had pledged that the U.S. would "return to normalcy" after the Great War, and now the Americans were again endeavoring to accomplish this feat. Millions of Americans had served overseas and massive governmental social engineering had transformed how citizens lived at home during the war. Servicemen and women were returning, and many Americans were attempting to remake the homeland into an ultranormal and deeply conservative society. For over fifteen years, the Great Depression and World War II had besieged the country, and now most citizens desired shelter from the war, pestilence, and economic collapse of the previous decade and a half. American society basked in the peace and prosperity of the postwar 1940s and 1950s, and its citizens attempted to redefine the country as an oasis of security and stability. Families grew as the baby boom soon created an ever-increasing population of children that reinforced the social appeal of the dependable nuclear family. The mythologized denizens of this age were middle-class families living in clean and well-maintained houses with well-manicured lawns in shiny new suburban neighborhoods. While many Americans did not actually live this way, this new ideal showcases what countless citizens desired from their society, namely strength, security, prosperity, and an emphasis on family. It also was what readers appeared to want from their comic book superheroes.

As Americans retreated to a seemingly safe and secure postwar existence, Superman and Batman also became ideal citizens and surrogate family men. The superduo had become patriotic protectors of the state during World War II and now needed to transition to the new postwar norm. The pair had little hope of returning to their Great Depression social avenger incarnations, which appeared no longer to be what society valued or needed. The comic book historian Bradford

W. Wright notes, "By appearances at least, the helpless and oppressed who had cried out for Superman in 1938 now lived comfortably and contentedly in the suburbs. Superheroes animated by the crusading spirit of the New Deal and World War II seemed directionless and irrelevant now that those victories has been won."[26] Americans had outlasted the Great Depression and won World War II, so why would they need superheroes to fight their battles? These social changes resulted in superhero comics losing many of their readers, and numerous comic book companies creating stories from other genres, including horror, romance, westerns, and crime. C.C. Beck, a Captain Marvel artist of the day, explained the postwar comic book transition by claiming that comic book heroes and heroines "…had nothing to do. They had become so humanized that they could no longer fly around, chase outlandish villains, or fight impossible monsters as they once had done; nobody believed in that fairy tale stuff anymore."[27] To make matters worse, critics like psychologist Fredric Wertham convinced many members of the public and several politicians that comic books stories were responsible for aberrant behavior among a number of young readers. In his 1954 book *Seduction of the Innocent*, Wertham claims that comic books are dangerous to children and adolescents, and states that Superman behaves as a fascist while Batman and Robin promote homosexuality. Largely because of detractors like Wertham, and the public backlash caused by an April 1954 United States Senate Subcommittee on Juvenile Delinquency hearing in which comic books were castigated, the comic book industry created a new self-regulation code in late 1954. The Comics Code Authority (CCA) set strict standards for what could and could not be published in comic book stories and pushed to remake the comic book industry into a wholesome reflection of 1950s American values. In reality, the code did not cause many changes at DC Comics because the publishers had self-censored the brand's comic books since the 1940s. What the CCA did was codify American social changes in comic book stories. No longer could superheroes be vigilantes or free spirits; a strict 1950s America would not allow it.[28] Superman and Batman now had little choice but to adjust to their new roles as pseudo-fathers and conservative agents of the state.

Superfamily Man

American society was recreating itself as a more conservative and secure place in the post-World War II 1940s and 1950s, and Superman and Batman were transitioning to their new, more socially conventional roles. During the war, Superman had quickly shed any of his remaining antisocial/vigilante ways, and in the postwar era the Man of Steel embraced his seemingly incompatible new roles as a more powerful hero and supercommon man. This seemingly oxymoronic existence greatly boosted Superman's superpowers, while turning him into a rather boring company man/father figure. To make Superman more exciting, creators increased his superabilities, thus allowing him to participate in exciting new adventures and to battle terrifying and world-threatening menaces and supervillains. Interestingly, Superman often used his enhanced powers for rather mundane tasks that appear to be an overall waste of his time. Why would an ultrapowerful individual worry about maintaining a secret identity, working a normal job, and cleaning his apartment? In order to make Superman more relatable and safe to worried parents and authority figures, comic book creators gave him a supernormal life. Writers and editors soon began to present the Man of Steel as a surrogate law enforcement agent while in costume and a blue-collar worker in his Clark Kent identity. Superman's supporting cast took a more prominent role and Lois Lane and Jimmy Olsen were quickly given comic books of their own, respectively subtitled "Superman's Girl Friend" and "Superman's Pal." This became the basis for the Man of Tomorrow's surrogate family, which before long also included the entire bottled miniature Kryptonian city of Kandor, a mermaid and former college girlfriend named Lori Lemaris, and a ménage of superpets including Krypto the Superdog, Streaky the Supercat, Comet the Super-Horse, and Beppo the Super-Monkey. In *Action Comics* #252 (May 1959), Superman discovers that he has a biological cousin who also survived Krypton's destruction. Kara Zor-El soon adopts the identity of Supergirl and the Man of Tomorrow serves as a fatherlike figure to the young Maid of Might. By the end of the 1950s, the once antisocial Man of Steel had secured state-sanctioned employment and family ties in both of his identities. Superman had once been a lone avenger fighting for justice but now he was a company/family man who extolled the virtues of postwar American life.

Unquestionably, the postwar story element that best exemplifies Superman's new status as a heightened version of a common 1950s American male is his often odd relationship with Lois Lane, his girlfriend. Lois Lane had been a part of the Superman mythos since the Man of Steel's first appearance in *Action Comics* #1, but had changed dramatically during her fictional lifetime. In early stories, Lois was a tough-minded and spunky career woman who could take care of herself, and showed little interest in Superman romantically. After the war, she changed dramatically though, and became obsessed with marrying the Man of Steel. In multiple tales during the 1940s and 1950s Lois tries to cajole, trick, or bully her way into becoming Mrs. Superman. A story in *Superman* #76 (June 1952) states, "No female in the history of the world–from Helen of Troy or Cleopatra right up to the No.1 glamour girl of the 20th century–ever pursued any man as determinedly as Lois Lane chases Superman! Every year is Leap Year as far as Lois' pursuit of Superman in concerned!"[29] Often Superman expends an inordinate amount of energy creating detailed ruses who make Lois look foolish and are frequently emotionally callous, even cruel. Superman generally treats Lois like a spoiled child that must be taught a number of life's difficult lessons. To make matters worse, when Lois is not trying to get Superman to marry her, she often is attempting to prove that Superman and Clark Kent are the same person. These two preoccupations waste a large amount of the Man of Steel's time, and shift the focus from fighting social wrongs and declaring his fervent nationalism to worrying about domestic issues and trying to stop any sort of personal or social change. The main goal of the Metropolis Marvel as a superhero had been to protect the innocent and right perceived wrongs. This has evolved and Superman now labors intently to preserve the status quo and wars against newness of any kind. Lois Lane provides an interesting foil who wants the Man of Steel to transform his life by getting married or revealing his dual identity. While Superman had once been an agent of change, in the postwar years he was now much too conservative and supernormal to even consider anything new. The Man of Steel was preoccupied with preventing alterations of any kind, be it social or personal. Superman believed that society had reached its pinnacle and any hint of transformation should be viewed with distrust. A hero who had once battled to remake American society now worked just as hard to prevent any type of change.

While Superman fought to guard his secret identity and struggled against Lois Lane's matrimonial entrapment efforts, he also protected the world from disasters and villains. During this period, many of his adversaries were low-level criminals that the Man of Steel could easily defeat while also worrying about Lois' newest scheme. Superman's more powerful foes were generally would-be world-conquerors and megalomaniacal madmen. Lex Luthor's responsibilities expanded, and the evil scientist soon filled the role of Superman's archnemesis. In the postwar era, the Man of Steel and Luthor rarely deviated from a socially acceptable script in which, in Act 1 and Act 2, the evil genius commits crimes or plans massive destruction, and then, in Act 3, Superman restores order and returns Luthor to his prison home. Interestingly, in the 1950s Superman stories, crime was not a choice or a byproduct of socio-economic/political conditions; rather it was an extension of evil, which was often portrayed as being genetic in nature. In other words, almost all of the criminals in these Superman tales are inherently evil and thus could not be rehabilitated or understood, but rather should only be stopped and incarcerated. This perception can be seen in a group of supercriminals from Krypton that Superman continually works to keep imprisoned in a "twilight dimension" known as the Phantom Zone. Although the Phantom Zone prisoners can theoretically be paroled, most are intrinsically immoral, cannot be reformed, and consistently vow revenge on Superman. This understanding of criminality worked well with postwar social norms that attempted to create a binary understanding of right/wrong and good/bad. Although Superman stories were produced in color, they were black-and-white interpretations for an America that generally did not tolerate deviant behavior. By the end of the 1950s, Superman had become a symbol of safety, security, and domestic tranquility. While earlier versions of the Man of Steel fought for social change, the postwar Superman worked hard to maintain American society's new conservative outlook. Superman was not the only hero who reflected this understanding though; Batman also had evolved after the war.

The Not-So-Dark Knight

Superman changed greatly after World War II in order to keep in step with postwar America's conservative needs and desires, and Batman followed the Man of Steel's lead. The Caped Crusader lost much of his formerly frightening image and instead became content to become a jovial and friendly costumed crime fighter. The hero who had once tried to scare and intimidate criminals was now a warm and inviting public servant beloved by both the government and the public at large. Like Superman, Batman also became the patriarch of an extended "family," which included Robin, Alfred his butler, Batwoman, Ace the Bat-Hound, and Bat-Mite (an imp from another dimension who idolizes the Dark Knight). After Fredric Wertham's allegations that Batman and Robin were homosexuals, female romantic interests were introduced into their stories in order to stress the Caped Crusader's heterosexuality.[30] These love interests did not take up as much of Batman's time as Lois Lane did Superman's though, and the Dark Knight and the Boy Wonder were mostly free to battle criminals and villains. Batman's rogues' gallery grew to include Calendar Man, Cluemaster, Killer Moth, and the Riddler. These often ridiculous and generally odd villains (and other previously introduced foes) presented opportunities for Batman to reinforce notions of socially acceptable behaviors, and to declare the rightness and justness of postwar beliefs and social norms. While Superman mostly fought intelligent scientists and would-be world-conquerors, Batman was mainly pitted against freakish villains who deviated from socially acceptable norms. The Dark Knight's rogues' gallery consisted of evildoers who celebrated their individuality and violated many of society's laws, rules, and customs. These villains were deviants in an America that did not accept such behavior, and Batman battled the bad guys' philosophies and outlooks as much as he did their criminal actions. The Caped Crusader could not risk the possibility that these ideas that violated understood social norms could become accepted and viable. Much like Superman, Batman's main task was to protect society from both internal and external threats, which included any changes that would upset the nation's delicate social equilibrium. According to these narratives, criminals wanted to change America but Batman (and Superman) understood that change would only cause unnecessary problems.

As an agent of the state, Batman worked to protect society's status quo and prevented criminals and villains from changing American life. The Great Depression and World War II had scarred many Americans, who wanted nothing more than peace and security, and the Dark Knight had become a clean-cut white-bread guardian of accepted social norms. This can be seen in many Batman stories from 1946 through 1959 that stress the fundamental rightness of the American social structure. An interesting example of an American myth-building Batman story can be found in the *Detective Comics* #205 (March 1954) story "The Origin of Bat-Cave." In this tale, Batman and Robin travel three hundred years into the past to better understand the inscription on a piece of Native American pottery. As soon as the Dynamic Duo arrive in the seventeenth century, the pair witness two Native American men on horseback chasing a European settler. Without taking time to understand the situation's background, Batman and Robin attack the Native Americans and save the white frontiersman. The twentieth-century crime fighters quickly learn that the settler is living in what will one day be the Batcave and has a dual identity of his own since he is masquerading as a Native American in order to learn the tribe's military and social secrets. Batman and Robin come to the pioneer's aid and redesign the cave to include seventeenth-century versions of many of the amenities that they will have in their future headquarters. These include a winch and pulley to lower the man's horse into the cave, a periscope, a trophy case to display souvenirs from his exploits, and a closet to hold disguises. The heroes soon dress up as Native Americans and infiltrate Huron society in order to help the European settlers. Batman and Robin save the frontiersman's life one last time and return him home before they are pulled back into the future.[31] Throughout the story the Dynamic Duo never question the underlying conflict or attempt to avoid tampering with the past. Likewise, the pair do not try to determine how or why the ill feelings originated, but rather instantly side with the European settler. The superheroes assume that the person whose appearance, background, and customs most resemble their own must be correct and should be protected. To question the frontiersmen would be to question the rightness of the future American society and express doubt about the postwar nation. The Dynamic Duo believed in a cultural hierarchy in which they were inherently superior to the settler, who was in turn culturally superior to the Native Americans. Batman and Robin's job was to protect the postwar U.S. even if they had to help create an understanding of the proper and innately superior postwar culture in the seventeenth century.

Batman and Robin's battles with their rogues' gallery also provided an opportunity for the crime-fighting-pair to express their devotion to postwar American society. Villains, by their very nature, are enemies of the state who wish to disrupt normal life and change the status quo. Batman's enemies were generally freakish and often grotesque individuals who flaunted their hatred of bourgeois norms and delighted in their refusal to submit to the rules and ideals that governed most Americans. This is certainly true of Batman's prime nemesis, the Joker, who became the Dark Knight's archenemy not long after the villain's debut in *Batman* #1 from the spring of 1940. The Clown Prince of Crime's criminal insanity served as a counter to Batman's rational, law-abiding nature that was well within the period's social norms. Like the Joker, many of the villains Batman fought were criminally insane and violated society's strict code of conduct. Perhaps the most socially revealing Batman villain of the time was Two-Face, a criminal whose very nature questioned the line between good and evil. The original Two-Face was District Attorney Harvey Kent, who became criminally insane after sulfuric acid had scarred his face in *Detective Comics* # 66 (August 1942). Once plastic surgery had restored Kent's appearance, he returned to a normal life. Later, in a story in *Batman* #68 (December 1951), a jealous boyfriend attacks the television actor Paul Sloane, who is portraying Two-Face, leaving half of the thespian's face horribly disfigured. The actor soon becomes criminally insane and assumes the vacated Two-Face identity. Sloan, like the original Two-Face, flips a silver-dollar coin to determine what criminal choices he will make and whether or not he will perform good or evil tasks. Like the villain's face, the coin features a scarred bad side and a normal looking good side, and after the coin is tossed the winning side mandates Two-Face's actions. The villain, who also expresses his duality by committing crimes that are linked to the number two, has little control of his actions. In this understanding, right and wrong are not choices but rather manifestations of one's physical and mental being. Sloane's deformation drove him insane and his mental state left him unfit to be a productive and successful member of society. Two-Face's aberrant appearance caused him to become an outsider and misfit in a society that tolerated neither.[32] This provides an enlightening Batman foil and showcases the Dark Knight's upstanding physical, mental, and moral nature. By the end of the 1950s Batman, like Superman, was not only a crime fighter but also a symbol of a prosperous and secure nation. The Dark Knight was the representation of a society that valued stability and conformity. Batman and Superman had changed greatly from the heroes they were created to be during the Great Depression. The pair were now symbols of a new era, but this would change again in the coming days.

Conclusion

Much like American society as a whole, Superman and Batman transformed greatly between 1938/1939 and 1959. The superduo were created to help Americans cope with the horror of the Great Depression and to be fictional instruments of social and political change. Superman battled street-level economic and social problems, while Batman often took on larger world-threatening menaces. The two heroes had to transition quickly to a World War II lifestyle and social understanding though, and before long they became superpatriots. The Man of Steel and the Dark Knight did their part to help the war effort and showed few signs of their past desires to remake society. Like many Americans during this period, the heroes were willing to do almost anything the government asked without question. The pair worked as war-bond salesmen and war-propaganda cover boys while seemingly happy to be of service to their troubled country. After the conflict was won, the two superheroes were expected once again to fall in line with the nation's desires and expectations. The country had suffered through over a decade and a half of economic hardship and war, and many Americans now desired a nation steeped in peace and security. A large number of citizens wanted a conservative and stable American society, which would serve as a salve for the preceding years' social and political wounds. Hidden under this society's safe and calm exterior was an undercurrent of fear that things would once again go wrong and the good times would end. Americans tried to enjoy their newfound wealth and security while fighting against both internal and external agents of change. In this environment, Superman and Batman became good-natured, law abiding, and frankly dull surrogate fathers. Like many American men, the superpair embraced their recently acquired adulthood and no longer attempted to fight authority; rather they came to represent the very authority that had once deeply troubled them. The superduo became symbols of America and this transformation brought with it the need for the heroes to mirror society in all of its conservative blandness. At the end of 1959, the majority of Americans were happy to be prosperous, secure, and uninterested in change, and they wanted Superman and Batman to also reflect these values. This would not last long though; there were dramatic social changes on the horizon that not even the nation's greatest superheroes could prevent.

Notes

1 Jerry Siegel and Joe Shuster. "Revolution in San Monte." *Action Comics* #2 in *The Superman Chronicles, Volume 1*. (New York: DC Comics, 2006): 17-30.

2 Siegel and Shuster. "Wanted Superman." *Action Comics* #9 in *The Superman Chronicles, Volume 1*: 112.

3 Siegel and Shuster. "Superman in the Slums." *Action Comics* #8 in *The Superman Chronicles, Volume 1*: 108.

4 *Superman Chronicles, Volume 1*: 110.

5 Although Batman was known as "the Bat-Man" early in his career, for consistency purposes this study will only refer to the character as the articleless and hyphenless Batman.

6 Bill Finger and Bob Kane. "The Case of the Chemical Syndicate." *Detective Comics* #27 in *The Batman Chronicles, Volume 1* (New York: DC Comics, 2005): 9.

7 Finger and Kane. "The Spies." *Detective Comics* #37 in *The Batman Chronicles, Volume 1*: 123.

8 Siegel and Shuster. "Superman vs. the Cab Protective League." *Action Comics* #13 in *The Superman Chronicles, Volume 1*: 185.

9 Siegel and Shuster. "The Economic Enemy." *Superman* # 4 in *The Superman Chronicles, Volume 3* (New York: DC Comics, 2007): 84.

10 Finger and Kane. "Introducing Robin, the Boy Wonder." *Detective Comics* #38 in *The Batman Chronicles, Volume 1*: 124-136.

11 Finger and Kane. "The Horde of the Green Dragon." *Detective Comics* #39 in *Batman Archives, Volume 1* (New York: DC Comics, 1997): 153.

12 Finger and Kane. "The Case of the Prophetic Pictures." *Detective Comics* #42 in *Batman Archives, Volume 1*: 179.

13 Finger and Kane. "The Land Behind the Light." *Detective Comics* #44 in *Batman Archives, Volume 1*: 193.

14 Siegel and Shuster. "The Slot Machine Racket." *Superman* #5 in *The Superman Chronicles, Volume 3*: 127-139.

15 Only issues of *Action Comics* were counted in these statistics. This is because *Superman* comics were a larger quarterly magazine that contained more stories and would have unfairly weighed the final tally.

16 Siegel and Shuster. "Superman's Super-Campaign." *Action Comics* #18 in *The Superman Chronicles, Volume 2* (New York: DC Comics, 2007): 128.

17 Cab Protective League." *Superman Chronicles, Volume 1*: 190.

18 Siegel and Shuster. "How Superman Would End the War." *Look Magazine*. February 27, 1940, in *Superman Through the Ages*. Accessed July 2, 2012. http://superman.nu/tales2/endsthewar/.

19 Brian Cronin. "Comic Book Urban Legends Revealed #49!" May 4, 2006. *Comic Book Resources*. Accessed March 8, 2012. http://goodcomics.comicbookresources.com/2006/05/04/comic-book-urban-legends-revealed-49/.

20 Siegel and Shuster. "America's Secret Weapon." *Superman* #23 in *Superman: From the Thirties to the Seventies* (New York: Crown Publishers, Inc., 1971):165.

21 *Thirties to the Seventies*: 173.

22 Don Cameron and Jack Burnley. "Swastika Over the White House!" *Batman* #14 in *Batman: The Dark Knight Archives* (New York: DC Comics, 2003): 97.

23 Cameron and Burnley. "The Two Futures!" *Batman* #15 in *Batman: The Dark Knight Archives*: 142.

24 *Dark Knight Archives*: 154.

25 Cameron and Burnley. "The Boy Who Wanted to Be Robin!" *Batman* #15 in *Batman: The Dark Knight Archives*: 129-141.

26 Bradford W. Wright, *Comic Book Nation: The Transformation of Youth Culture in America* (Baltimore: Johns Hopkins University Press, 2001): 59.

27 C.C. Beck. "Captain Marvel and the Atomic War." *DC's Greatest Imaginary Stories*. (New York: DC Comics, 2005).

28 David Hadju. *The Ten-Cent Plague: The Great Comic Book Scare and How it Changed America* (New York: Picador, 2009).

29 Michael L. Fleisher. *The Great Superman Book* (New York: Warner Books, 1978): 411.

30 Andrew Wheeler. "The Gayness of Batman: A Brief History [Opinion]." April 30, 2012. *Comics Alliance*. Accessed May 12, 2012. http://www.comicsalliance.com/2012/04/30/the-gayness-of-batman-a-brief-history-opinion-morrison/

31 Finger and Leonard Star. "The Origin of the Bat-Cave." *Detective Comics* #204 (New York: DC Comics, March 1954).

32 Finger and Charles Paris. "The New Crimes of Two-Face." *Batman* #68 (New York: DC Comics, December 1951).

Fig. 0.3
A young Superman fan appreciates the Man of Steel's exploits in 1942. U.S. Farm Security Administration/Office of War Information, Library of Congress, 1939

CHAPTER 2

Middle Age Changes

On January 20, 1961, John F. Kennedy took the oath of office and became the thirty-fifth President of the United States. The young leader delivered a speech that day which symbolically marked a paradigm shift. Kennedy famously stated,

> Let the word go forth from this time and place, to friend and foe alike, that the torch has been passed to a new generation of Americans—born in this century, tempered by war, disciplined by a hard and bitter peace, proud of our ancient heritage—and unwilling to witness or permit the slow undoing of those human rights to which this nation has always been committed, and to which we are committed today at home and around the world.[1]

Although President Kennedy claimed that things had changed, in reality the 1960s began in much the same way the 1950s had ended. American society remained seemingly prosperous, safe, and bland, while battling hidden fears of the unknown. Superman and Batman continued in their roles as wholesome agents of the state who embraced their young adulthoods and no longer resembled the wild adolescents they had been only a few years earlier. The two heroes were now symbols of a rigid and fearful society that wanted to avoid major changes; they had to act accordingly. Society was slowly changing though, and what most citizens did not sense was that within a few short years the American cultural and social landscape would become almost unrecognizable. The baby-boom generation would soon fight for social control, and before long the seemingly safe, secure, and harmonious America of the 1950s would be a distant memory. As American society transformed, the older generation that had fought World War II needed to determine how to proceed. Should the generation's citizens adjust to the new times, fight for their ideas and try to preserve the society they had built, or just ignore the changes and hope that things would eventually return to what they considered normal? This is the problem that Superman and Batman also faced during the mid-1960s. To many young baby boomers, the superpair would come to represent the repressive and fear-laden values of the "Greatest Generation." Like many Americans, Superman's and Batman's creators had to decide what to change and what to keep the same.

Weisinger's Worries

The first few years of the 1960s America closely mirrored the country during the 1950s. Citizens continued to value security and stability at the expense of freedom and self-expression, and America worked hard to forget the horrors of the Great Depression and World War II. Superman and Batman also remained solid 1950s-style superheroes as they labored to protect the status quo and diligently fought against change in all of its various forms. The two superheroes were now national symbols and thus were tied to adult society's wishes, which made the heroes successful, but it also made them vulnerable to alterations in taste and demographics. The longtime editor Mort Weisinger continued to shape the Superman mythos during the 1960s. Because the editor generally supplied writers with story plots, it was Weisinger who was primarily responsible for expanding Superman's surrogate family, increasing the Man of Steel's power levels, and making the hero the supernormal version of the stereotypical average 1950s American male. Like American society, Weisinger's seemingly pacific Superman stories contained an undercurrent of fear and distrust. During the 1950s and 1960s Superman would often find himself temporarily transformed in grotesque and horrifying ways. In a typical tale, the Man of Steel would become old, overweight, or malicious because of some convoluted plot device. Numerous comic book professionals and scholars have claimed that these stories are the results of Weisinger's unconscious fears that were revealed to his psychiatrist during therapy sessions.[2] In essence, Weisinger was using Superman stories to expose the dark side of 1950s and early 1960s America. The editor's 1960s Superman showcased a powerful hero who was also deeply worried about the world around him. These words also could be used to describe American society itself.

Mort Weisinger transferred his own fears and insecurities to 1950s and 1960s Superman stories, which helped to make the Man of Steel a credible representation of a conservative and fearful American society. In a May 4, 1970 article in the *Reading Eagle*, Weisinger states "… Superman gave me a gross inferiority complex. He utterly frustrated me. I couldn't stand shining in Superman's reflected light. I was his satellite, and I wanted to be the sun. I couldn't bear it when people bragged about knowing me only because of my connection with him. I kept on trying to compete with him."[3] These fears and frustrations can be found in numerous stories and comic books from the Weisinger era. One of Weisinger's most often-used storytelling devices was a mysterious piece of Superman's birth world called red kryptonite. A story in *Action Comics* #283 (December 1961) describes red kryptonite as ordinary kryptonite that "went through a strange cosmic cloud… Ever since then, red kryptonite always had peculiar, unpredictable effects on Superman!"[4] If Superman was a symbol of American society, then red kryptonite was a representation of unknown menaces that could wreak havoc and destroy security and normality. In a series of tales, Superman is exposed to red kryptonite and has severe nightmares, becomes a toddler, grows long hair and fingernails, splits into an evil Superman and good Clark Kent, turns into a space monster, develops the head and antennae of an ant, transforms into a giant, finds his face changing colors depending on his mood, and loses his superpowers on one half of his body. Almost all of these stories were written and drawn between 1960 and 1964, and it appears as if fear and paranoia were overcoming both Weisinger and Superman. The decade had changed but on the surface the first few years of the 1960s were very much like the 1950s. Superman was still incredibly powerful and conservative, but his underlying fears were starting to get the better of him.

Fantastical Batman

Much like Superman, Batman continued to display the same characteristics at the start of the 1960s that he had at the end of the 1950s. The Caped Crusader had also expanded his pseudo-family while battling small-time crooks and extravagant villains. The formerly gritty and frightening Caped Crusader transformed into a cheery costumed nice guy who endeavored to preserve a safe, secure, and friendly American society. Many of his early 1960s tales included elements of the fantastic, and forced the Dark Knight to fight on alien planets, in strange dimensions, and in many odd environments in which his street-level crime-fighting skills seemed misplaced. Batman was now a conservative protector of the status quo who was forced into situations for which he was not designed. Examples of this abound, but one of the most interesting of these fantastical 1960s stories is in *World's Finest* #113 (November 1960) in which Superman and Batman fight Bat-Mite and Mr. Mxyzptlk, two ultrapowerful pests from other dimensions. Bat-Mite and Mr. Mxyzptlk are not villains in the traditional sense of the word, but rather annoyances who threaten society's normalcy. The two are playful menaces who endanger Americans' safety and security. Because their powers can literally change any aspect of society, the pair serve as the stereotypical postwar threat. This is highlighted in the story's first page in which Batman states, "Superman, we'll have to stop this silly duel of theirs!" and Superman replies, "Right, Batman! If they don't stop using their powers on each other, they'll turn the city topsy-turvy."[5] The issue highlights the lengths to which Superman and Batman will go to stop any sort of change or unpleasantness. The most telling demonstration of the superpair's assistance is when the antagonists spill maple syrup in the street and Superman remarks, "And I'll have to clean it all up, with a touch of my superpowers, before the streets become like a strip of flypaper."[6] The Man of Steel then stands on his head in the middle of the spill and uses his "steel-strong hair as a mop… [to] scrub up every spot of this sticky mess."[7] Superman and Batman now could not bear to allow any kind of social disruption or annoyance, no matter how minor, to affect American society. The superpair went to great lengths to prevent even the most infinitesimal example of deviancy. The two heroes swallowed their pride and performed outlandish acts in ridiculous stories in order to protect their homeland. The two would do almost anything to prevent even the slightest degree of change.

Another story that displays the inane tales about conformity in which Batman regularly appeared during the early 1960s is *Batman* #153 (February 1963), "Prisoners of Three Worlds." This odd adventure features Batman, Robin, Batwoman, and Bat-Girl battling an alien that steals silver in order to fund a would-be alien dictator. At one point in the story, Batman and Batwoman's energy essences are transported to another planet while their corporeal selves remain on Earth. As the elder crime fighters are split into two entities, Robin and Bat-Girl are sent to a different world where they battle against an alien menace from the "dimension of doom." In *Batman* #134 (September 1960), Batman and Robin travel to South America and square off with a "rainbow creature" covered in stripes of red, blue, yellow, and green. Each of the color stripes produces a different superpower that causes a large amount of societal damage until Batman and Robin destroy the menace. *Batman* #136 (December 1960) showcases space aliens that have taken over a U.S. town in preparation for an upcoming invasion. The story stresses that the town's citizens supposedly hate Batman and Robin, a seemingly impossible fact because the bat-team's place in society would prevent such a belief. In *Batman* #140 (June 1961), the Dynamic Duo transform into space aliens after returning from an interplanetary mission. The two heroes briefly possess the power to create tidal waves but are predictably returned to normal by the issue's end. Perhaps the oddest Dark Knight story is featured in *Batman* #147 (May 1962) in which the Caped Crusader de-ages and becomes a costumed toddler known as "Bat-Baby." These peculiar stories underscore the notion that even the most trivial and benign changes were viewed as threats to the established social order. Batman could not allow anything to evolve no matter how insignificant the action might seem. Much like the proponents of George Keenan's Cold War containment theory, the Caped Crusader worried about what would be the end result of the first domino falling. Batman had to protect American society from all changes, no matter how inconsequential, because no one could know what even a small action might lead to and the Dark Knight wanted things to remain just the way they were.

Perhaps the most famous story from this period is "Robin Dies at Dawn" featured in *Batman* #156 (June 1963). The popular tale is not actually as silly as the aforementioned stories, but is rather odd, and showcases American society's deep-seated fear during this time. In the story, Batman takes part in a secret military sensory-deprivation experiment designed to better understand the negative effects of isolation. While participating in the experiment, Batman has a mental breakdown and begins suffering from powerful nightmarish hallucinations. During one of his delusions the Dark Knight believes that Robin has been murdered on another world and that he could do nothing to prevent it. This unimaginable scenario so thoroughly exhausts Batman mentally, and incapacitates him, that the Caped Crusader retires and turns over his crime-fighting responsibilities to Robin.[8] Although Batman returns to his rightful role by the end of the story, it is important to note that for a time Batman has such serious mental problems that he can no longer perform his crime-fighting duties. One can argue that a grown man who dresses up like a bat to avenge his parents' murders already suffers from mental instability, but within the context of superhero mythology let us assume that Batman is generally sane. If so, then Batman's mental breakdown is truly exceptional because it reveals a fragile public servant who fears he is not powerful enough to protect his surrogate family. The fear of Robin's death incapacitates Batman and ultimately defeats the Dark Knight in a way that no supervillain ever could.

By the early 1960s, Batman was no longer dark and terrifying, but rather had become a helpful and protective father figure who suffered monthly abuses that often left him deformed and battered. Month after month the Dark Knight was transformed into another grotesque version of himself, and although he seemingly returned to his normal persona by story's end, his psyche could only take so much damage. Like the majority of Americans, Batman was much more delicate than most would believe. The world was changing and he was trying to keep up, but the constant physical and mental abuse was taking its toll. The 1950s had been a seemingly peaceful and quiet decade that concealed a large amount of inner fear and turmoil. In June 1963, these societal terrors had temporarily broken the Dark Knight, and although he quickly adjusted, it was obvious that he was in fact fallible. Soon many Americans' worst fear would also come to pass and the nation itself would have to adjust to a new paradigm. The seemingly safe postwar era was coming to an end and Batman, for one, seemed worse for the wear.

A Whole New World

Many would argue that although the decade had officially commenced a few years earlier, the social and cultural 1960s began on November 22, 1963. Most people will recognize this as the date that Lee Harvey Oswald assassinated President John F. Kennedy in Dallas, Texas. On that day, the peaceful and secure society that the World War II generation had worked so hard to build was irrevocably transformed. Although it would take years for many of these changes to come to fruition, the United States would never again be the same, and many American citizens would spend decades trying to regain the perceived postwar innocence. Superman and Batman did not officially comment on President Kennedy's death (although an "In Memoriam" page appeared in *Superman* #168 and a later story from July 1964 (*Superman* #170) did showcase the Man of Steel taking a special mission from the president.) Like much of the country, the superpair mourned silently as they continued to perform their daily tasks, but change was coming whether they liked it or not. As the baby boomers were maturing, they were beginning to demand new types of cultural narratives and outlets that were strikingly different from the 1940s and 1950s versions. In February 1964, the Beatles would appear on *The Ed Sullivan Show*, showcasing how American popular music needed to shift to meet the new generation's wants and needs. Film, television, literature, and other media would soon follow suit as the cultural and social 1960s were commencing. As had previously happened at the end of World War II and in the postwar period, comic books were also changing to meet cultural and social demands. By the start of 1964, a vibrant, revitalized competitor utilizing a novel comic book esthetic had appeared upon the scene, and Superman and Batman's keepers once again had to decide how to meet this new challenge. Marvel Comics had arrived and the new comic book company would prove to be a bigger threat than any villain had ever been.

During the 1950s, DC Comics became the primary superhero comics publisher in the United States. Although other companies attempted to battle DC for market share, none succeeded at dethroning the comic-book-publishing powerhouse. By 1960, DC was selling at least the market's top twenty superhero titles and no other publisher seemed poised to threaten the company's stronghold on the genre.[9] Unexpectedly, this began to change when Marvel Comics published *The Fantastic Four* #1, cover dated November 1961. DC had long cornered the market on safe and respectable superheroes, whose good manners and white-bread ways appealed to parents and other authority figures alike. In contrast, Marvel's titles, beginning with *The Fantastic Four*, embraced a new, more youthful narrative which seemingly rebelled against established norms and welcomed a new, less restrictive culture. DC's characters were affable, good-natured, and reputable citizens who fought against external threats. By contrast, Marvel heroes were flawed characters who struggled against internal (figurative) demons and battled themselves and other heroes as often as they warred against supervillains. By the early 1960s, Superman and Batman had come to represent everything that parents and society wanted children to be, respectful, hard-working, polite citizens who followed the rules and were in turn happy in their daily lives. These DC heroes faced few problems that could not be solved in one short story. Spider-Man, the Incredible Hulk, the Fantastic Four, and other Marvel heroes led a much different fictional existence. Although these new characters fought crime and supervillains in a traditional manner, they also exhibited real world fears and problems that made them identifiable to young and adolescent readers. Spider-Man lived with guilt over his role in his uncle's death while battling financial problems and schoolyard bullies. The Incredible Hulk was a lonely outcast whom society hated and misunderstood. The Fantastic Four were a bickering superfamily that seemed to fight among themselves as much as they solved problems or encountered supervillains. These heroes with "feet of clay" appealed to many younger baby-boomer readers, while Superman and Batman remained super-role models from an older generation.

Batman's New Boss

As Marvel Comics created heroes with personalities and problems that attracted numerous baby-boomer readers, DC continued to produce mostly light-hearted and silly Superman and Batman tales. Superman-related stories remained popular and continued to outsell the most-read Marvel titles by a wide margin in the early and mid-1960s.[10] Marvel was creating new and interesting superhero stories but Superman's safe adventures still reigned supreme at the newsstand. Unfortunately Batman's adventures were not selling as well and there were rumors that DC editors wanted to cancel the Dark Knight's comic books or perhaps do something even more drastic. Batman-creator Bob Kane claimed that "they were planning to kill Batman off altogether."[11] Instead of ending the Caped Crusader's adventures, DC Comics management turned over the Batman editorship to longtime writer and editor Julius Schwartz. The new editor had recently revitalized numerous older DC superheroes by creating new modern versions of these often outdated characters. Schwartz's efforts were so successful that he is credited with starting a new comic book era known as the Silver Age, which would last until the 1970s. (The Golden Age of comic books is partitioned to include the original superheroes from the 1930s and 1940s.) DC management hoped that Schwartz could rejuvenate Batman's stories and increase the Caped Crusader's poor sales. Schwartz noted, "I took over Batman, which I didn't want to do, but they said I had to because the magazine was doing badly. I wouldn't say they were going to kill it, but it certainly was being discussed."[12] Comic book historian Les Daniels notes that Schwartz changed three basic things about Batman: "... He abandoned the policy of putting Batman through freakish transformations, he jettisoned all references to aliens and outer space, and he unceremoniously banished the dependent members of the 'Batman family,' including Bat-Hound, Bat-Mite, Bat-Girl, and Batwoman. It was as if they never existed..."[13] The new editor attempted to emphasize Batman's role as crime fighter and detective, and story elements that were not in keeping with this understanding were quickly and completely scrapped. The twenty-something-year-old Batman was getting a face lift but it was unclear if readers would approve of these new cosmetic changes.

The first Julius Schwartz-edited Batman story appeared in May 1964's *Detective Comics* #327. Reportedly, when Schwartz became the Batman editor, DC publisher Irwin Donenfeld told the new Batman boss, "It's simple: Batman is dying. I'm giving you two guys six months to fix it. If not, it's over."[14] The other guy in Donenfeld's statement was a young and innovative artist named Carmine Infantino. As indicated by this proclamation, Infantino's art and overall influence was a large part of Batman's reconstruction. The new Batman tales featured a more contemporary art style most apparent in Infantino's pencils and his understanding of how pages should be rendered for maximum storytelling potential that would appeal to a more sophisticated audience. Older Batman stories had featured a more cartoony art style, but Infantino, and often the inker Joe Giella, produced more natural and realistic representations that are most apparent on his bold and engaging cover art. Besides the general art style, the most obvious change that Schwartz made was to redesign Batman's costume symbol to include a black bat inside of a bright yellow oval chest emblem that replaced the Dark Knight's former solitary black bat insignia. This new eye-catching logo was a reflection of the growing and influential pop art movement that, ironically, had taken many of its ideas from comic book and strip drawings. Artists like Andy Warhol and Roy Lichtenstein borrowed heavily from comic book influences, and now Batman aesthetics were in turn mirroring an enhanced version of comic book gaudiness.

A Darker Knight

While Batman's tales featured modern designs and brightly colored costumes, the stories were darker and more mysterious than in the previous decade. New Caped Crusader adventures focused more on Batman's detective skills and reintroduced a number of villains from the Dark Knight's extensive rogues' gallery. Costumed bad guys like the Riddler, Mr. Freeze, and the Joker once again battled the Caped Crusader as Schwartz's Batman focused more on action and mystery than the superhero's previous incarnation. This new tone and concentration is evident from the beginning of *Detective Comics* #327, the rejuvenated series' first issue under Schwartz's leadership. The opening text box at the top of page reads, "It was a strange power that top crook Frank Fenton wielded over **Batman** and **Robin**! No sooner would the pair come within sight of the startling criminal than they'd be rendered completely helpless—unable to make a move against him! Follow the tangled clues of the gripping story which leads through the most picturesque quarter of **Gotham City**... and builds to a fantastic climax!" (bold in the original).[15] This opening reads more like the prose of a Raymond Chandler detective novel than a Batman comic book story. The Dark Knight was now focusing more on his detective skills and was no longer fighting aliens or magical beings as he had in the previous years. The Caped Crusader was suddenly an adventuring crime-fighting detective who utilized both physical force and brainpower to battle crime and right wrongs, and thus his new stories borrowed elements from both hard-boiled detectives and swashbuckling heroes. This marked an attempt to return to more serious and complex stories as American society was transitioning to better meet the baby boomers' desires, and to face a litany of new challenges. Batman was attempting to recreate himself for an evolving society, but it was still unclear if a return to his detective roots combined with pop art influences was what readers demanded.

Like many good crime stories, new 1964 Batman tales also asked social and moral questions that cannot be quickly or easily answered. Although Batman's artistic style was bright and colorful, the stories themselves contained numerous dark elements and many morally grey areas that contrasted with the previous era's black-and-white understanding of the Caped Crusader's comic book world. In the aforementioned *Detective Comics* #327, the second page opens with text that suggests to the reader that some social and political questions are not easily answered even in a Batman comic book story. The lead text reads, "In the middle of modern **Gotham City** lies an **anachronism**, a relic of the past! Some call ancient **Gotham Village** a festering wound at the heart of the bustling metropolis! Others term it a historical landmark and valuable living area! Who is right?" (bold in the original).[16] Although the story's end reveals one side's leader to be a criminal using his position for corrupt purposes, it still contains a gritty ambiguity rarely seen in over two decades of

Batman stories. This introductory tale features all of the elements of Schwartz's new detective-centered style. Besides tying into the previously addressed social issues, the story's main criminal also provides a physical problem and a mystery for Batman to solve. The foe has the amazing ability to paralyze Batman and Robin and stop the Dynamic Duo from thwarting his criminal activities. Through a series of clues, Batman is eventually able to understand and combat the criminal's mind-control technique. The issue ends with the Dark Knight capturing the bad guy, explaining how he solved the mystery, and providing a happy ending for almost everyone involved. The new Batman was proving himself to be cerebral, athletic, and adventurous, which afforded the opportunity to produce innovative types of stories. A new, more sophisticated audience demanded that the Caped Crusader be updated to meet society's ever-shifting desires. Baby boomers were creating a new cultural identity and Marvel's heroes were altering the comic book landscape. Batman was transforming in order to meet society's needs, but before long he would have to change again.

There are numerous examples of 1964 and 1965 Batman stories that display the Dark Knight's new gritty, cerebral detective outlook. Although this reconstituted Batman would only exist for a short time, DC creators produced over two dozen comic books containing his adventures. These stories featured a serious and intellectual Batman who used science and technology to fight crime in a dark urban environment. In these tales, nefarious villains abound and Batman often appears to be the lone force that prevents evil from flourishing and polluting a decent moral society. In June 1964's *Detective Comics* #328, the Dark Knight defeats the villainous Tri-State Gang while in the next month's *Detective Comics* #329 the Caped Crusader appears in a gothic tale in which he overcomes death traps in an English castle in order solve a case linked to Nazi war-crimes treasure. Perhaps most interesting is *Detective Comics* #332 (October 1964) in which Batman fights the Joker for the first time under the new creative regime. In this story the Clown Prince of Crime creates a potent dust that causes anyone it comes in contact with to laugh uncontrollably. After encountering the drug, Batman researches possible cures and learns that a simple antihistamine will stop the uncontainable laughter. The Caped Crusader soon thwarts the villain's evil plans and protects society from the psychopathic clown. This version of Batman is portrayed as being clearly more intelligent and cunning than his archnemsis, but the Joker is also more nefarious and crafty than he had been in recent appearances. By contrast, in a February 1965 story in *Batman* #169 the villain known as the Penguin is reintroduced into the Dark Knight mythos. The umbrella-carrying and top-hat-wearing criminal attempts to steal a jewel-encrusted meteorite before Batman and Robin foil his evil plans. The Caped Crusader had become a better detective and a more serious crime fighter, but his foes still varied from street gangs, to psychopathic clowns, to farcical parasol-carrying thieves. Many of these Julius Schwartz-edited Batman stories were far-fetched and sometimes puerile while focusing on the Dark Knight's detective skills, but each tale showcased the Dark Knight as a renewed, more serious crime fighter. Batman was a much different superhero than he had been just months before, but to keep up with social needs he would soon have to change yet again. By 1966, television would transform Batman into something that comic book readers had never seen before.

Changes and Riddles

Julius Schwartz's detective-focused Batman lasted roughly from May 1964 until February 1966. During this less-than-two-year time period the series attempted to revitalize the Caped Crusader but ultimately gave way to another more socially accepted direction. Throughout this period Schwartz and his writers and artists not only updated Batman's appearance and changed the comic book's storytelling methods, they also briefly killed Batman's butler and trusted associate Alfred Pennyworth and replaced the manservant with Dick Grayson's Aunt Harriett. The snooping Harriett was supposed to be a motherlike figure to Bruce Wayne and Dick Grayson who added femininity and supervision to the two men's world. (DC executives and editors were still very cognizant of Fredric Wertham's allegations that Batman and Robin were homosexuals and wanted to use Aunt Harriett to counter such claims.) Aunt Harriett would only exist in Batman stories for a short time though, and before long Alfred would return from the dead and again become a vital part of the comic book mythos. Arguably the most important story that would appear during this period was in May 1965's *Batman* #171. The tale entitled "Remarkable Ruse of the Riddler" is the villain's first appearance in over fifteen years. As his name would suggest, the Riddler is obsessed with puzzles and questions, and commits crimes related to this mania. The story begins with the question-mark-sporting costumed criminal being released from prison and seemingly helping Batman and Robin capture a group of bad guys. Throughout the tale, the Riddler tricks the Dynamic Duo into believing that he is committing crimes that turn out to have simple noncriminal explanations. Eventually though, it is revealed that the Riddler was leaving clues for the superpair, while he was planning and executing a major crime. Ultimately Batman and Robin solve the puzzle and the Riddler is sent back to prison, where he reveals the answer to one final riddle. The story showcases how

Batman and Robin use their detective skills to work out the Riddler's puzzles, and their physical prowess to prevent him from committing further crimes.[17] In many ways, the blending of the cerebral and the corporeal in this story exemplified the focus on Batman stories during the early years of Julius Schwartz's editorship.

The Riddler story in *Batman* #171 is important not only because it reflects a typical 1964/1965 Batman story but also because it served as a bridge from the Dark Knight's detective phase to his next incarnation, which began in 1966. In December 1964, Hugh Hefner threw a party at the Playboy mansion in Chicago at which he screened the low-budget 1943 Batman serial. An ABC Television executive was at the soiree and loved the low-budget film so much that he began developing a Batman television show. The Batman series would be purposely campy while combining humor and action/adventure. The actor and producer William Dozier was put in charge of producing the new show and one of the executive's first tasks was learning about Batman and Robin's history, narrative tone, and style. Dozier had no background knowledge of the Dynamic Duo and had to quickly learn everything he could about the superheroes. The producer remembers, "I scurried around and bought maybe seven or eight different vintage copies of the Batman comic books, and felt like a fool doing it. I read them—if that is the word—and asked myself, 'What do I do with this?' I thought they were crazy. I really thought they were crazy if they were going to try to put this on television."[18] Reportedly one of the comic books that Dozier bought was *Batman* #171, featuring the Riddler's story. Interestingly, although the story displayed Batman and Robin's detective skills, it also relied heavily on numerous over-the-top plot points and story details. The Riddler's green and purple question-mark-covered costume, the silly clues and puzzle-themed death traps, along with a number of groan-inducing jokes, gave the story a less-than-serious tone. The creators of the Batman television show would adopt and heighten this fun-loving attitude and would embrace the campiness that was inherent in many comic book stories. The television show's first episode would use a script based on the Riddler story in *Batman* #171, but would change the tale to better meet a different audience's perceived needs and desires.[19] Batman had transformed into a detective-centered crime fighter only a short time before, but now he was already preparing to transition again. This time the Caped Crusader would become hipper and trendier in order to attempt to satisfy society's desires. As Batman was changing greatly though, Superman was staying mostly the same.

Still Superman - 1964–1969

As low sales and new social standards and desires forced DC's editors and creators to renovate Batman's persona, Superman remained predominantly the same. While American society was changing drastically, the Man of Steel appeared to be a conservative island of stability in a turbulent sea of social and cultural transformation. As the baby boomers demanded that society become more youth-centered, fashion, music, and multiple other forms of entertainment adjusted to meet these desires. In the comics industry, Marvel Comics created new, hip superheroes who better reflected a younger generation of readers. Likewise, DC refashioned new versions of many 1930s and 1940s heroes who were more relatable to young fans. As rock and roll was changing music, free love and drug use were transforming social norms and destroying old taboos, and the counterculture was remaking American life, one thing remained the same: Superman. The Man of Steel served as a stalwart traditional icon that would not sway or waver, even during the cultural upheaval which would redefine the nation during the 1960s. Buoyed by strong comic book sales, Superman became a symbol of either classic American wholesomeness and nostalgia, or an oppressive outdated Cold War philosophy that had become archaistic, depending on one's point of view. The Man of Steel was a litmus test for how a given American might feel about self and country. Superman remained unchanged as the nation around him was undergoing drastic transformations, and because of this the Man of Steel became an excellent lens through which to view the world. As the youth-culture revolution took hold, Superman endured as an unchanging and unrepentant symbol of what once had been an open question as to what the country should look like.

The 1960s was a decade of change, especially in the United States. Political, cultural, and social transformations redefined the country as the young baby boomers attempted to assert a greater level of control, often much to their parents' and grandparents' chagrin. The 1960s were such a multifaceted period that it is impossible to describe cleanly and concisely all of the numerous battles and social alterations which were taking place. Following John F. Kennedy's death in 1963, young Americans became more and more disenchanted with the country. Protesters demonstrated against racial inequality, the American military's participation in Vietnam, and a litany of other perceived injustices. Assassins murdered not only President Kennedy, but also his brother and presidential candidate Robert Kennedy, along with civil rights leaders Martin Luther King, Jr., and Malcolm X. Riots erupted in the street as police officers battled youthful protesters, creating a highly symbolic confrontation between the authority of the older generations and the desires of the newer. Young Americans began dressing, grooming, and acting in nontraditional ways while listening to new music and discussing counterculture ideas that encouraged a break from conventional thinking and practices. Many Americans were dissatisfied with their country and their ways of life, and, as the decade progressed, this frustration only appeared to grow. Free love, drug use, and a litany of new alternative understandings of social and political systems seemed to many to offer solutions to a stagnant and repressive American society. Many young Americans were demanding these changes, as numerous older Americans could not understand what was wrong with society, and blamed the younger generation for creating this chaos. As with most historical surveys, this is an overly simplistic retelling of the time's events, but the latter half of the 1960s generally witnessed battles between the agents of change and those who wanted little or no drastic reform. Inside these binary black-and-whites were endless shades of gray beliefs and opinions, but most Americans could have been shoehorned into one of these two camps. As these traditionalists and reformers battled for the United States' future, Superman remained the domineering moral progovernment force that he had been throughout the late 1940s, 1950s, and early 1960s. The Man of Steel was clearly happy with society and did not want anyone including its citizens (and his readers) to change it.

Not a Sunshine Superman

Jerry Siegel and Joe Shuster created Superman in the 1930s, and his Great Depression heritage clearly separates him from the baby boom generation that would follow. Like the generation that grew up in the 1930s, Superman distinctly bears the scars of having survived economic hardship and war. His 1950s and 1960s persona displays the authoritarian and conservative stance of a seemingly confident America, who secretly battles his hidden fears that one day the chaos will return. While Superman's readers were mostly children, the Man of Steel was not a baby boomer hero, but rather he remained the older generation's icon. During the 1960s, Superman outsold every other superhero comic book except in 1966 and 1967, when the Batman television series buoyed the Caped Crusader's sales. Even though newer, more modern heroes were closing the gap each year, in 1969, Superman's supporting cast member Lois Lane's comic book was still outselling Spider-Man, Marvel's top-selling superhero. Superman was the comic book personification of the establishment, and to many was a solid voice of reason in a world gone mad. Marvel Comics creators parodied Superman's traditional stuffy image in *Not Brand Echh* #7, a *Mad* magazine-style comic book that produced satirical narratives about social and cultural trends and icons. In the story entitled "The Origin of Stuporman," published in April 1967, the writer and artist portray the Superman proxy, Stuporman, as a white-bread American icon who helped to win World War II before signing a deal with a large comic book publishing company. The comic book creators and publisher soon make Stuporman insanely powerful, surrounding him with a large "family" and a menagerie of superpowered animals. In this parody, the corporate men have robbed the Superman stand-in of his uniqueness and made him a boring superpowerful family man, a shell of the hero he once was. At the end of the story, Stuporman casts out DC's editors and all of the other superheroes, and seemingly has his comic book world to himself again, like in 1938. Unfortunately he soon finds that the Marvel heroes have invaded his world and are declaring the start of a new era.[20] In seven short pages, "The Origin of Stuporman" showcases both Superman's conservative nature and the outdated changes that had followed the character since the 1950s. The story contrasts the traditional-minded Superman with the modern Marvel heroes, and displays how many comic book readers in particular, and baby boomers as a whole, viewed the Man of Steel. The original superhero has become a proxy for what many members of the younger generation saw as wrong with the United States: too conservative, too powerful, and too greedy. This seemed to matter little to DC Comics staffers though; Superman was not changing even if the Marvel heroes and many of the baby boomers were making fun of him.

Superman's desire to remain a traditional icon can be seen as a reflection of the character's age and his creator's past experiences. In 1968, Superman turned thirty years old and had survived many more physical catastrophes, political changes, and social upheavals than the newly popular Marvel heroes that now surrounded him. Numerous stories showcase the late-1960s Superman steadfastly clinging to his traditionalism and refusing to bow to social and cultural pressure. Some of the most interesting present Superman as a strong-minded parental figure and sometimes an arrogant jerk. Many of these comic books featured covers in which the Man of Steel is acting gleefully rude or exceptionally insensitive and then, inside the comic book, the story reveals that Superman is right to do so in fact. These narratives can be seen as metatextual declarations from Superman to the baby boomers, pronouncing that the Man of Steel (and by extension the older generation) knows best and occasionally the younger generation needs this super-tough love. While the Marvel heroes were the reader's friends, Superman was a stern 1950s father/authority figure who often had to teach children and young adults much-needed lessons. Unsurprisingly, the two characters that most often benefited from Superman's stern guidance were Jimmy Olsen and Lois Lane. Creators generally portrayed the young *Daily Planet* reporter Jimmy Olsen less as "Superman's pal" than as a naïve young man in need of direction and leadership. Likewise Superman often treats Lois Lane more like a child than a love interest, and consistently finds it necessary to teach her lessons about how she should act. Although Lois and Superman are seemingly contemporaries, the Man of Steel regularly has the need to prove that he is more intelligent and all-around superior to his "girlfriend." Superman had displayed this kind of behavior throughout the 1950s and early 1960s, but by the closing years of the latter decade, the Man of Steel seemed more defensive and authoritarian and less playful. When taken in context, it seems as if Superman was obliged to battle against a rapidly changing world and assert his dominance over the new generation. Lois and Jimmy now personified baby boomer excesses and missteps, and the Man of Steel promptly became the stern, out-of-touch older adult. Superman's understanding and views regarding his place in society remained the same even if the world around him was changing, and the Man of Steel did not seem to like this at all.

Old Superman

As Superman aggressively protected his traditional 1950s self, Lois Lane and Jimmy Olsen began to distance themselves from their superfriend. Although the stories often reveal different narratives, in 1968 and 1969 the covers of *Superman's Pal, Jimmy Olsen* and *Superman's Girl Friend, Lois Lane* display an ongoing battle between the Man of Steel and his two friends. This continuing skirmish mirrors the day's social paradigm and reflects the generational conflict inherent in 1960s society. Like many in the generation that fought World War II, Superman was fighting against change, while Lois and Jimmy represented the baby boomers who desired new social and cultural experiences. One of the most telling of these covers is from *Superman's Girl Friend, Lois Lane* #80 (January 1968), which features a metatextual image of Lois literally destroying her comic book's status quo. The Neal Adams drawn image features a stylish Lois Lane ripping the words "Girl Friend" from the comic book's cover as she fights with Superman. The obviously angry Lois yells at a stunned Man of Steel, "Get out of my magazine, Superman! I'm leaving Metropolis to start a new life… one that doesn't include you." The issue's story contains a narrative in which Lois leaves Superman because he has forgotten her birthday, but by the end of the issue he partially wins her back.[21] The cover displays a strange mixture of aggression and misunderstanding between loved ones which expertly expresses the period's dominant sentiment. The younger generation was attempting to tear down existing social norms much as Lois rips apart her link to Superman. The older generation (like the Man of Steel) was stunned by the anger and vitriol that seemed to them to be childish and undeserved. On another telling cover, *Lois Lane* #85 (August 1968), Lois is shown lifting a large boulder-sized chunk of kryptonite over her head as she peers down at a seemingly weakened and scared Superman. The Man of Steel states, " Great, Lois. Now heave that rock into space... then we'll start planning our wedding." To this Lois replies, "This kryptonite boulder can destroy you, Superman, but to me it's as harmless as a soap bubble! Because now I'm more super than you!"[22] Because it was produced in the U.S. in 1968, it is difficult not to read this cover as a commentary on change in America. Superman represents the older generations and is pressing to protect the status quo, while Lois is a change-minded baby boomer. Superman offers his "girlfriend" the thing that she has long wanted (marriage) in exchange for her obeying his dictates and directions, much as the older generation told the baby boomers to follow society's rules in order to become happy and prosperous. Superman, the symbol of the older generation, is obviously much weakened and in a vulnerable state. Lois, like the baby boomers, has become much more powerful and no longer wants the things that she once thought she did. Lois not only refuses the Man of Steel's offer, but is angered that he does not understand that he no longer controls her as he once did. Much like the younger generation, Lois is beginning to display her newfound power and authority, and Superman can do little to prevent this. As the decade closed, Superman was still a popular traditional icon, but it was obvious that not even he could win the fight against change. The Man of Steel was refusing to evolve, but this stance was becoming more and more quixotic as the decade progressed.

Bat Camp

While Superman spent the 1960s battling change and attempting to reinforce traditional social and cultural notions, Batman seemingly embraced change and transformed himself numerous times during the tumultuous decade. As previously noted, much like Superman, the Caped Crusader began the 1960s as a conservative superhero who fought against space aliens, magicians, and numerous other types of bizarre and silly foes. After Julius Schwartz took over the editorship helm in 1964, the Dark Knight became a more serious crime fighter who relied on his detective skills to battle criminals and costumed villains. Batman remained this way until 1966, when the character again dramatically assumed a new incarnation. The aforementioned Batman television show debuted on ABC on January 12, 1966, and quickly became a nationwide phenomenon. The series, written in a pop-art camp style, emphasized the juvenile strangeness of a grown man dressed as a bat fighting odd costumed villains. The Batman show appealed to both children on an action/adventure level, and adults, who enjoyed the playful campy fun. Adam West and Burt Ward starred as Batman and Robin, and numerous Hollywood actors, including Vincent Price, Cesar Romero, Eartha Kitt, and Joan Collins, appeared as villains of the week. The goofy show was a massive hit and soon Batmania was rampant, as Batman-related stories and merchandise flooded the market. DC Comics editors knew that this type of publicity was too good to pass up, and before long the comic book stories began to mirror the television in both style and tone. The comic book Batman would now become the silly campy version of himself that television viewers seemingly preferred.[23] Ironically, the comic book Batman had changed from a more light-hearted character only a few years before. This sudden reversal showcases DC Comics editors' and publishers' willingness to follow social trends and update the Dark Knight in order to remain current, well respected, and popular. This differed from their approach with Superman mainly because the Man of Steel's sales remained strong throughout most of the 1960s, while Batman's readership numbers were much lower. In the short term, the decision to model the comic book Batman after his television counterpart paid dividends as *Batman* rose from the ninth best-selling comic book in 1965 to number one in 1966. During this period, sales increased from 453,745 to 898,470, almost two times as much.[24] In 1966, the Batman television series was wildly popular, and suddenly, so was the comic book version. Unfortunately, quickly developing fads often end just as rapidly as they begin.

In 1966 and 1967, Batman comic books rode the wave created by the television show's popularity. Sales increased substantially and the character seemed to be at the center of the nation's consciousness. Dark Knight stories from this time reflect the television series' dramatic style and colorful palette. Batman and Robin discarded their more serious tone for what most comic book professionals understood would be short-term sales gains. Julius Schwartz, the editor of Batman, noted, "I don't know if I was with it, but it was the thing to do. When the television show was a success, I was asked to be campy, and of course when the show faded, so did the comic books."[25] Nonetheless, comic book stories focused on often silly dialogue and ridiculous plot twists that were akin to the television show's style. One plot point that ran for several months was the resurrection of Bruce Wayne's butler, Alfred Pennyworth. The English gentleman servant had died in June 1964, so that the feminizing presence of Aunt Harriett could be introduced into the Batman mythos. Because the Batman television show wanted to include Alfred, Julius Schwartz and company quickly had to find a way to return the butler to the Batcave. This was undertaken by fashioning a villain known as the Outsider who would later be revealed as a criminally insane Alfred. It was eventually discovered that Alfred had not been killed but rather was in a deathlike trance. A scientist discovered the catatonic manservant and used an experimental ray in an attempt to revive Batman's former employee. The treatment did indeed resuscitate Alfred but also turned him into the evil Outsider, a villain with telekinetic powers and a hatred of Batman and Robin. Eventually the Dynamic Duo battle the Outsider in *Detective Comics* #356 (October 1966) and restore their trusty butler to good health and good standing.[26] The Outsider stories reveal the campy attitude of the day as the creators emphasize how outlandish and over-the-top that Batman stories could be. Television viewers seemingly enjoyed the funny, playful, juvenile Caped Crusader, and the comic book changed to fit these new criteria, although the stories often seemed overly processed and unnatural. The television series set the standard for the comic book and often this turned into a campy mess, but at least one good thing came from this arrangement: Batgirl.

Meet Batgirl

The Batman television show began as a popular serial that attracted millions of viewers for each of its twice-weekly episodes. By its third season, the series was slipping in the ratings though, and producers were searching for novel ways to attract new viewers. Enlisting the aid of a beautiful woman is a time-honored method of attracting attention, and television executives requested that the Batman comic book team create a new female character who could be used on the series. Julius Schwartz, Carmine Infantino, and the rest of the crew designed a new Batgirl, a very different character from the Bat-Girl of an earlier era. The 1950s-era Betty Kane Bat-Girl was little more than a potential love interest for Robin and often a way for young male readers to tremble at the notion of the Boy Wonder being trapped into a relationship with this "yucky" girl. Bat-Girl allowed Robin to demonstrate his heterosexuality safely without surrendering his freedom or compromising his bachelor status. The 1950s Bat-Girl, along with the Kathy Kane Batwoman, reinforced the notion of male social superiority. Batwoman and Bat-Girl were debutants who played at crime fighting, and Batman and Robin were often forced to protect the two costumed women from the dangers of the world around them. The two superheroines seemed to worry more about romantically entrapping the Caped Crusaders than actually fighting crime. Much like Lois Lane and her relationship with Superman, the Batwoman and Bat-Girl characters demonstrated to young male readers that women were chiefly worried about finding a romantic bond that would eventually lead to marriage. Because women were so concerned with matters of the heart and other domestic activities, they could not be trusted with more substantial tasks, and should instead be pampered and placated. This understanding of gender relations was acceptable (and even encouraged) during the 1950s and early 1960s, but was no longer socially relevant in the latter part of the '60s. Instead, the new Batgirl would have to have far different qualities than her domestically minded predecessor. The redesigned Batgirl would have to be acceptable to a new generation of men and women who viewed gender roles very differently from older Americans.

The new Batgirl first appeared in *Detective Comics* #359 (January 1967) in a story written by Gardner Fox and penciled by Carmine Infantino. The innovative superheroine was clearly very different from her earlier counterpart in both appearance and outlook. Batgirl's modern, stylish black costume and her take-control attitude quickly made her a favorite of many comic book readers of the day. One DC fan noted in a published letter in *Detective Comics* #417 that the original Batwoman and Bat-Girl "...were there because romance seemed to be needed in Batman's life. But thanks to the big change and a foresighted editor, these hapless females are gone for good. In their place stands a girl who is a capable crime-fighter, a far cry from Batwoman who constantly had to be rescued from Batman."[27] The new Batgirl is Barbara Gordon, the daughter of the police commissioner James Gordon. The exceptional young woman holds a PhD in library science and works as the director of the Gotham City Public Library. While the earlier Bat-Girl was a female version of Robin who served as Batwoman's sidekick, Dr. Gordon is portrayed as an independent and capable woman who does not need a man to fulfill her. Rather, Batgirl fights crime out of a sense of civic duty, and because she craves adventure; she does not have the desire to romantically nab either Batman or Robin. Instead, Batgirl is a scarlet-haired symbol of women's changing roles within Batman's stories. Batgirl may have been created for television viewers, but soon she became a comic book staple. While some of her early adventures were still campy and silly, her debut displayed the vast changes that had taken place between the beginning of the 1960s and the decade's end.

Batgirl Stories

Batgirl's first appearance in January 1967 features the heroine's origin story, in which it is revealed that Barbara Gordon is on her way to a costume party, dressed as Batgirl, when she sees Killer Moth and his gang attempting to rob Bruce Wayne. Batgirl battles the criminals long enough for Bruce Wayne to slip away and change into Batman, although Killer Moth manages to get away for the time being. Gordon declares to herself that this will be the only time that she fights crime as Batgirl, but eventually she realizes that she craves the thrill and adrenaline rush. By the end of the story, Batgirl returns to costumed superheroics and helps Batman and Robin apprehend Killer Moth. Batgirl's origin may seem sophomoric to modern readers, who might doubt that a young untrained woman could fight crime on a whim, but the new superhero proves herself to be very capable in this narrative. Batgirl demonstrates her intelligence, her mastery of judo and other fighting skills, and performs well under pressure while both fighting criminals and being questioned by Batman and Robin.[28] In Batgirl's second adventure, in *Detective Comics* #363 (May 1967), the new superheroine deciphers a library-related code that allows her to help stop a gang of thieves. In this story, Batgirl is highly qualified and repeatedly displays her mental and physical prowess. Batman even trusts the masked Barbara Gordon to play along with a ruse in which he falsely reveals his secret identity in order to ensnare the criminals.[29] Most importantly, even during these first two appearances, Batgirl is portrayed as Batman's equal, not a sidekick, superfan, or possible love interest. Batman does not intimidate or overshadow the librarian-turned-hero; instead Batgirl acts like a self-assured woman, who believes that she belongs alongside one of the world's greatest superheroes. Batgirl is a heroine for a new era, a strong, sophisticated, and skillful superwoman, a characterization that would have been unthinkable only a few years before. While Batman's adventures followed the television show's campy example during these two plus years, the Dark Knight's stories also change to meet new social norms. Batgirl's creation was the best thing that came from Batman's puerile television stories, and showed how much the Caped Crusader's narratives were adapting to an ever-changing American society.

Decade's End

Batgirl has remained popular for decades after her introduction; the same cannot be said for the Batman television show. The series suffered from low ratings during its third season, and its last episode aired on March 14, 1968. The once fashionable show had lasted just over two years, and by 1968 most Americans considered it merely another passing fad. Unfortunately, the Batman series' lasting legacy was that many Americans equated the show's campy and colorful style with all comic book narratives. This misunderstanding of comic books still resonates with many citizens well into the twenty-first century. Few comic book professionals had liked the campy television-show-style Batman, but the company had decided to cash in on the short-term marketing and sales bonanza. After the Batman-market bubble burst, it was time for Julius Schwartz, Carmine Infantino and other DC Comics staffers to recreate Batman yet again. The campy television Batman was no longer acceptable (if he ever had been to most comic book fans) and the storytellers did not want to return to early detective Batman stories as if nothing had happened. Batman needed a new direction once again, and the character had to distance himself from his recent failure. Batman had to transform into a new version of himself while keeping his core identity. The Dark Knight needed to shed the parts of his identity that were no longer desirable and find the ideal Batman for this era. Batman's identity crisis is very much in keeping with the changes that were taking place within American society as a whole. As the Caped Crusader struggled with discovering his true self, Americans were attempting to redefine themselves and their society. Old ideas were being cast away and new understandings introduced. Strangely, a comic book character that fought crime dressed as a bat mirrored this social and cultural turmoil.

It is ironic that the comic book character Batman mirrored the 1960s' social and cultural reconstruction. As students protested the war, baby boomers experimented with drugs, free love, and rock and roll, and long-held values and mores changed, Americans searched for answers. Superman, the hero who originated in the 1930s as a populist social reformer, showed no signs of introspection or transformation during the 1960s. The Man of Steel refused to internalize the nation's identity struggles. Batman, on the other hand, is a millionaire who wishes to force his own morals and ethics on society by fighting crime. He is the prime example of a member of the privileged elite imposing his will upon the needy masses. In this understanding, it is ironic that Batman, an agent of stratified capitalism, more easily succumbs to society's whims and wishes. Batman is modeling society's need for change, while Superman attempts to provide a stabilizing force, which runs counter to the growing call among much of the populace for social modifications. It was Batman's lack of readership which forced or allowed for these changes and which permitted the Dark Knight to restructure himself to better meet new social understandings and needs. Julius Schwartz and company began to renew Batman once again in August 1968, when the Dark Knight's official creator, Bob Kane, signed a new contract that greatly reduced his role as a member of the character's creative team. As Batman's originator, Kane would still be paid but would no longer provide any story ideas or artwork. Other Kane-era staffers like Sheldon Moldoff were also essentially terminated and DC brought in several new writers and artists.[30] Interestingly Schwartz and his crew replaced long-time storytellers in an effort to return Batman to the dark and serious tone that was present during the character's inception in the 1930s. New writers like Frank Robbins and Bob Haney joined artists that included Irv Novick, Bob Brown, and Neal Adams in creating a new Batman for a period that would eventually become known as the Bronze Age. These stories, produced from mid-1968 through 1970, paradoxically display a sharp break from the previous campy era, but also showcase a Batman in transition and not entirely the dark and moody knight that he would be during much of the 1970s. Batman writers and artists had to repair the Caped Crusader's tarnished campy image and these early Bronze Age stories began the process.

Batman's creative team had little time to transform the Dark Knight's image before the end of the decade, but several stories that ran in two comic books known as *The Brave and Bold* and *World's Finest* served as a template for changes that would be realized in the coming years. In the last two years of the 1960s, artist Neal Adams began drawing Batman in the aforementioned comic book titles, both of which had Batman teaming with either Superman or another DC superhero in every issue. Most of the stories were fairly traditional tales written either by Bob Haney or Leo Dorfman, but Adams' art provided a dark and mysterious feeling to many of them. Adams' drawings displayed a gritty and human Batman who seemed to continuously fight his way through pain and hardship. Adams' Caped Crusader wars against criminals, fights against society's dark nature, and struggles unremittingly through a thick fog of grime and corruption. This is a Dark Knight true to his name. In *The Brave and Bold* #79 (August/September 1968), Adams draws a gaunt and gloomy Batman as the Caped Crusader teams with Deadman, a ghost who can inhabit living human's bodies for a brief time period. Adams' artwork transforms this conventional tale of murder and secrets into something jarring and novel. Suddenly, Batman is a creature of pain and anguish, and no longer only a billionaire dressed in a bat costume. The Dark Knight is not merely a detective and crime fighter, but also a tormented and lost soul searching for closure and redemption.[31] Adams' pencils produce the same outcome in the next issue, *The Brave and the Bold* #80, in which the insane crime fighter the Creeper joins the Caped Crusader. Because comic books are a visual storytelling medium, Adams' page layouts, realistic human likenesses, and other artistic techniques create a dark and sinister tone rarely seen in previous comic books. The tale becomes irregular and unsettling, inviting the reader to follow the pair through Gotham's muck and grime.[32] These Adams narratives preview adjustments in Batman storytelling that would not come to fruition until Adams himself teamed up with scribe Denny O'Neil in the early 1970s. During this transition period, most Dark Knight stories were fairly predictable narratives, as writers worked to regain their footing after moving from campy to serious tales and only Adams' exceptional artwork showcased the novel Caped Crusader who would shortly appear. Another Batman change was in the offing, and at the end of the 1960s, Neal Adams was providing readers with the coming attractions.

Conclusion

The 1960s were a decade of unprecedented social and cultural upheaval. Citizens of the United States struggled to redefine and recreate their understanding of the concept of America. While the older generations labored to preserve the elements of society that they held dear, the young baby boomers pressed to remake their homeland into what they believed was a fairer and more equitable nation. As the two sides battled to construct their versions of a better America, the country faced the grave challenges of war, political assassination, racial and gender inequality, and numerous others. The United States was changing in a rapid manner that the nation had not experienced before or since. As these changes were debated, discussed, and argued against, Superman and Batman also entered the fray. While neither of the two superheroes openly pushed for or against the 1960s social and cultural change, the two heroes did fall on different sides of the divide. Superman, the original superhero, stayed true to his Great Depression roots and refused to modify his conservative outlook. If anything, the Man of Steel's traditionalist nature only intensified as he attempted to teach the baby boomers his life lessons regarding proper conduct, manners, and behaviors. Superman remained a superconservative who endeavored to protect a 1950s-style American society throughout the 1960s, even as the counterculture proved this stance to be untenable. Batman, on the other hand, spent the 1960s open to the idea of change, as showcased by his numerous transformations during the decade. Much like Superman, Batman began the 1960s as a conservative superhero who was a proud defender of the status quo. Throughout the decade, the Dark Knight changed often, though, and the crime fighter attempted to transform himself to meet the public's new needs. As Superman strove to lead by example, Batman worked to be what the majority of Americans wished him to be. From conservative hero, to cerebral detective, to campy goofball, to the start of a dark and brooding knight, Batman changed into what Americans seemed to want. Batman was the surrogate baby boomer while Superman served as the symbolic older generation. Both heroes served the U.S. but in far different ways. As the 1960s ended, Superman and Batman still struggled to understand the world around them and the way forward. In this way, they were the perfect guardians of an America in which the citizens were uncertain about the present and worried about the future. Superman and Batman could not save Americans from their problems but they could provide some relief from the growing storm.

Notes

1 John F. Kennedy. Inaugural Address. January 20, 1961. *The American Presidency Project*. Accessed May 12, 2012, http://www.presidency.ucsb.edu/ws/index.php?pid=8032.

2 Gerald Jones. *Men of Tomorrow: Geeks, Gangsters, and the Birth of the Comic Book* (New York: Basic Books, 2004): 190-191.

3 Norton Mockridge. "This Wonderful World." *Reading Eagle*. May 4, 1970. *Google News*. Accessed June 17, 2012, http://news.google.com/

4 Michael L. Fleisher. *The Great Superman Book* (New York: Warner Books, 1978): 372.

5 Jerry Coleman and Bernard Bailey. "Bat-Mite Meets Mr. Mxyzptlk." *World's Finest Comics* #113 (New York: DC Comics, November 1960).

6 Coleman and Bailey. "Bat-Mite."

7 Coleman and Bailey. "Bat-Mite."

8 Finger and Sheldon Moldoff. "Robin Dies at Dawn." *Batman* #156 (New York: DC Comics, June 1963).

9 "1960 Comic Book Sales Figures." *The Comics Chronicles*. Accessed May 17, 2012, http://www.comichron.com/yearlycomicssales/1960s/1960.html

10 "1965 Comic Book Sales Figures." *The Comics Chronicles*. Accessed May 17, 2012. http://www.comichron.com/yearlycomicssales/1960s/1965.html.

11 Les Daniels. *Batman: The Complete History* (San Francisco: Chronicle Books, 2004): 95.

12 Daniels. *Batman*: 95-97.

13 Daniels. *Batman*: 97.

14 "Secret Origins of the Batman TV Show, Part One! Batman Begins." *Dial B for Blog*. Accessed May 18, 2012, http://www.dialbforblog.com/archives/204/.

15 John Broome. "Mystery of the Menacing Mask." *Detective Comics* #327 (New York: DC Comics, May 1964): 1.

16 Broome. "Mystery": 2.

17 Gardner Fox and Carmine Infantino. "Remarkable Ruse of the Riddler." *Batman* #171 (New York: DC Comics, May 1965).

18 "Secret Origins." Accessed May 18, 2012.

19 Daniels. *Batman*: 103.

20 Stan Lee and Sol Brodsky. "The Origin of Stuporman!" *Not Brand Echh* #7 (New York, Marvel Comics, April 1967.)

21 Neal Adams. Cover image. *Superman's Girl Friend Lois Lane* #80 (New York: DC Comics, January 1968.)

22 Neal Adams. Cover image. *Superman's Girl Friend Lois Lane* #85 (New York: DC Comics, August 1968.)

23 Daniels. *Batman*: 114.

24 "1966 Comic Book Sales Figures." *The Comics Chronicles.* Accessed May 17, 2012, http://www.comichron.com/yearlycomicssales/1960s/1966.html.

25 Daniels. *Batman*: 114.

26 Gardner Fox and Carmine Infantino. "Inside Story of the Outsider." *Detective Comics* #356 (New York: DC Comics, October 1966.)

27 Fred Grandinetti. "Remembering Kathy Kane: The First Batwoman." *Newsarama.* Accessed June 27, 2012, http://web.archive.org/web/20070929132840/http://www.newsarama.com/dcnew/Batwoman/BatwomanHistory.htm.

28 Gardner Fox and Carmine Infantino. "The Million Dollar Debut on Batgirl!" *Detective Comics* #359 in *Showcase Presents: Batgirl, Volume 1* (New York: DC Comics, 2007): 8-23.

29 Gardner Fox and Carmine Infantino. "The True False-Face of Batman." *Detective Comics* #363 in *Showcase Presents: Batgirl, Volume 1* (New York: DC Comics, 2007): 24-39.

30 Daniels. *Batman*: 117.

31 Bob Haney and Neal Adams. "The Track of the Hook." *The Brave and the Bold* #79 in *Batman Illustrated By Neal Adams* (New York: DC Comics, 2003): 55-79.

32 Bob Haney and Neal Adams. "And Hellgrammite Is His Name." *The Brave and the Bold* #80 in *Batman Illustrated By Neal Adams* (New York: DC Comics, 2003): 83-106.

Fig. 0.4
The March 11, 1966 *Life* magazine cover showcased Batman for a nation in the grips of "Batmania." Joel Yale Time & Life Pictures Getty Images.

CHAPTER 3

The Early 1970s—Self Doubt and Worry

The great baseball philosopher (and catcher) Yogi Berra once famously said, "You got to be very careful if you don't know where you're going, because you might not get there."[1] Many Americans entered the 1970s not knowing where they were going, and afraid of where they might end up. The 1960s were a decade of unprecedented political, social, and cultural changes that were introduced so quickly that the country scarcely had an opportunity to adjust. New cultural and social understandings came out of clashes regarding civil rights, war protests, gender and sexual norms, and other challenges to traditional American standards and values. As the specter of the Vietnam conflict haunted society, Americans attempted to define themselves and the new rules that governed their lives. The U.S. homeland was no longer the World War II generation's attempt at a safe and homogeneous society. Instead, many Americans invited disorder and change, while others battled against these new ideas. This, along with several political and economic events and challenges, turned the 1970s into a dark decade filled with adversity, distrust, and decline. While Americans were redefining themselves and adjusting to their new realities, Batman and Superman were also becoming darker and more reflective. The heroes had to adjust to life in a society that often no longer believed in itself or its mythical protectors. Many Americans were losing their sense of patriotism and exceptionalism, a major blow to comic book characters who had long come to identify themselves with the nation and its symbolic trappings. During the early 1970s, Superman and Batman themselves had to become more self-doubting and jaded, just as many Americans were. New stories appeared who questioned the heroes' very natures and purposes, and by inference questioned the country itself. By the decade's midpoint, the nation had seen a president resign in disgrace, the military disengage from a bloody conflict that had lasted over ten years, and the country embroiled in an energy crisis and economic recession. By 1975 the country that only a decade before had appeared prosperous, peaceful, and safe was seemingly descending into turmoil and apathy. Superman and Batman walked a fine line of trying to encourage Americans while also mirroring the bad times troubling the nation. The dark days were here for both normal and superpowered Americans alike.

Dark Dark Knight

Like many Americans, Batman ended the 1960s searching for a new identity and trying to readjust to a rapidly changing society. Comic book creators began to emphasize the Caped Crusader's mysterious and threatening side by casting him in darker and more earnest tales. These stories served to distance the Dark Knight from his campy past and to emphasize that this version of Batman should be taken seriously. In retrospect, these tales also provided a transition from the silly mid-1960s Batman to the truly dark and moody Caped Crusader who was to come. Although writers and artists like Frank Robbins, Bob Brown, and Dick Giordano created serviceable stories that returned Batman to his precamp days, these tales offered little that was new and inventive. The Batman stories from mid-1968 to 1970 place our hero in an updated version of a 1930s hardboiled detective story. While earlier 1960s tales allowed Batman to display his detective skills as a street-level superhero, these new stories turn the Caped Crusader into a neo-Sam Spade in a world filled with dames, corruption, and sinister plots. Batman was more supergumshoe than superhero. This changed dramatically in January 1970 when writer Denny O'Neil teamed up with artist Neal Adams on *Detective Comics* #395. This was O'Neil's first foray into writing the Dark Knight, although, as noted above, Adams had drawn several previous Batman covers and stories. The O'Neil/Adams (or Denny O'Neal Adams, as the pair was sometimes nicknamed) story serves as a dividing line for all that had come before and all that would soon be. It showcased what Batman would become during the 1970s, and also provided a cultural lens through which to view that decade as one of uncertainty and hostility.

Gothic Batman

Detective Comics #395 contains a story entitled "The Secret of the Waiting Graves" which challenged many well-established Batman conventions and set the foundation for a new era of storytelling. Writer Denny O'Neil noted that his approach to Dark Knight narratives took a particular color, "I just wanted to make 'Batman' Gothic and spooky. I was being influenced by writers like Lovecraft and Poe, and I didn't think about Gotham City."[2] "The Secret of the Waiting Graves" resembles a Mexican horror film more than it does a superhero comic book or detective story. The plot features Bruce Wayne traveling to Mexico to attend a party thrown by an eccentric wealthy couple. Only moments after he arrives, Batman must rescue another guest from attacking falcons, and soon two wolves are hunting the Dark Knight himself. Eventually the Caped Crusader learns that his hosts, Juan and Dolores Muerto, are over a century old because of a special plant with hallucinogenic properties which keeps them youthful. It is revealed that the blossom (known as the Sybil flower) causes powerful visions which eventually drive the affected party into madness. Towards the story's end, Batman has to save a federal agent's life, overcome terrifying hallucinations, fight falcons to escape a death trap, and destroy the Sybil flowers before they can cause the world harm. The issue concludes with the Muertos rapidly aging and dying, because the special flora no longer provides immortality, and Batman writing the year of their deaths on their tombstones. O'Neil and Adams leave many storytelling gaps that often force the reader to reread passages and search for clues in order to understand why Batman acts in given ways. The narrative also uses a much different tone and pacing than most other Dark Knight tales, and this unto itself leaves the reader on edge and searching for a context in which to understand what is happening. These things cause the reader to remain off balance and places both Batman and his fans outside their normal comfort zone, thus creating a sense of anxiety and eventually horror, which makes the tale's plot elements even more powerful.[3]

"The Secret of the Waiting Graves" is interesting for both what it contains and what it does not. The story focuses chiefly on a wealthy couple who are trying to kill a government agent in order to protect a powerful secret. The only criminal acts that take place are assault and attempted murder, crimes that are generally too minor for Batman's notice. The Caped Crusader is not in Gotham City (or even the United States), and there is little evidence that he is in Mexico investigating a crime. Batman does not battle an adversary to reacquire private property, to assert American nationalism, to prevent standard criminal activity, or to stop a devious plot. Rather, the Dark Knight is drawn into a situation in which two possibly insane individuals possess a powerful weapon that could wreak havoc if unleashed on the world. Batman is taking a proactive, preventive stance to counteract possible future problems. No threats have been made, though, and there is no evidence of plans to use the weapon; rather Batman is worried about what could happen, not what he knows will happen or has happened. This is quite a contrast to how Batman (and most law enforcement) normally operates. Generally the Cowled Crusader chases criminals who have committed a crime, or have left irrefutable evidence that they have plans to perpetrate criminal activities. Here Batman indicates that he will no longer abide by those limitations and will instead redefine both himself and his understanding of crime. Neal Adams' groundbreaking artwork emboldens and reinforces these story points. Adams' realistic renderings of human beings, his inventive page layouts and viewpoints, and his artistic storytelling techniques were like nothing seen before in comic book art. Adams' influence can still be seen in a legion of comic book artists' work, but in the 1970s, his drawings were revolutionary. O'Neil's stories and Adams' art propelled Batman in a much darker and sinister direction. The pair worked together on only sixteen *Batman* and *Detective Comics* issues, and seven stories in *The Brave and the Bold*. The duo's influence is unparalleled during this era, though, and this is especially true if their stories are compared to the work of other Batman creators at this time. Denny O'Neil and Neal Adams were producing groundbreaking Batman stories that were pushing the Dark Knight in a new direction. Much like society, Batman was exploring new social understandings and was entering a dark period. The Caped Crusader no longer followed the same rules and guidelines as before, just as many Americans were transitioning to a new perception of themselves and their country.

Denny O'Neil and Neal Adams produced only a handful of the Batman stories published in 1970 and 1971. Frank Robbins, Bob Brown, and Irv Novick provided the story and art for most of the other Dark Knight tales. These stories were close in tone and style to the transitional tales of late 1968 and 1968, but were also slowly becoming darker and grittier as the months passed Neal Adams' art influenced Brown's and Novick's styles, and Robbins explored deeper understandings of crime and Batman's psychological makeup. These Bronze Age Batman tales closely mirror many of the Hollywood movies of the era, in which lone antiheroes battle against madmen, crime, and other social ills in an attempt to save society from itself. Clint Eastwood, Charles Bronson, and a plethora of other actors portrayed motion picture vigilantes who worked to clean up a corrupt and apparently disintegrating society. In the past few years, Americans had watched as assassins killed national leaders, tens of thousands of servicemen died in Southeast Asia, young people rioted in the street, and the country's historical values appeared to be under assault. To make matters worse, the economy was suffering a downturn and a host of new social problems loomed on the horizon. Batman had not yet become as dark and menacing as the celluloid vigilantes, but he was on his way. Americans were suffering, and they needed a hero who could suffer alongside them and maybe find a way to help them solve some of their problems. Batman appeared to be up to the challenge. Many comic book readers also wanted Superman to adapt to the current social situation, but it was unclear if he would be able to give his fans what they desired. The Man of Steel could do almost anything except change.

Seventies Superman?

As the 1970s began, Batman was once again adjusting to new

social and cultural needs, while Superman was fighting against these changes by continuing to be the conservative hero he had been since the 1950s. The Man of Steel remained defiant even as American society continuously adapted. By 1970, Superman was not only the last son of his dead planet Krypton, but also the final 1950s-style superhero who refused to accept new social conventions and realities. Batman, other DC heroes, and all the Marvel characters remained works in progress who transformed quickly and often. Superman's refusal to compromise had caused him not only to fall behind, but to border on archaic. The Man of Steel was the middle-aged conservative who was stuck in the 1950s, even as the world around him constantly reformed itself. Superman was so old-fashioned that he was becoming a joke among comic book fans and social commentators, who often saw him as a quaint remnant from a long-gone time. One well-known example of this criticism is Larry Niven's amusing 1971 essay "Man of Steel, Woman of Kleenex." In this piece, Niven seemingly seriously considers Superman's identity and sexual problems while also implying that modern readers need the Man of Steel to act differently than he has in the past. Niven implies that Superman has to adjust to a society that wants to openly discuss sexuality and neurosis, and by clinging to an antiquated moral code, the Man of Steel is not fulfilling his responsibilities as a hero and an icon. Americans expected a closeness with their heroes that was no longer available with Superman. Marvel superheroes shared their problems, failures, and successes with the reading public. These new heroes tore down boundaries and allowed comic book fans to understand them as flawed human beings. Superman did not do this; rather he continuously presented himself as a nearly perfect protector, which made him increasingly hard to identify with. Many comic book readers, and much of the American public, wanted their superheroes to act like friends who openly shared their problems and weaknesses. Instead of opening up, Superman remained a repressive father figure who sternly lectured his followers and refused to change even as he was becoming increasingly irrelevant.

Larry Niven's "Man of Steel, Woman of Kleenex" offers interesting insights into Superman's place in American society in the early 1970s. The author views the comic book icon through the lens of a 1970s America that was growing disillusioned with the nation's direction. A generation that had lived through the radical 1960s now faced a plethora of problems, many of which seemed to have no solution. By focusing on Superman's sex life and potential personal problems, Niven is attempting to place the Man of Steel in the same context as other members of an American society who had grown and evolved. In the first paragraph the author states, "The purpose of this article is to point out some medical drawbacks to being a [K]ryptonian among human beings, and to suggest possible solutions.

The [K]ryptonian humanoid must not be allowed to go the way of the pterodactyl and the passenger pigeon."[4] Niven then proceeds to outline how difficult having sex and children with his human girlfriend, Lois Lane, would be for the Man of Steel. The author states the couple would experience numerous problems based on Superman's Kryptonian physiology. Superman would seemingly be unable to control himself during intercourse and would probably harm Lois during a period of intense pleasure. Regarding this, Niven writes, "Lastly, he'd blow off the top of [Lois's] head. Ejaculation of semen is entirely involuntary in the human male, and in all other forms of terrestrial life. It would be unreasonable to assume otherwise for a [K]ryptonian. But with [K]ryptonian muscles behind it, Kal-El's semen would emerge with the muzzle velocity of a machine gun bullet."[5] Niven goes on to detail how Lois Lane would not be able to give birth to a half-Kryptonian baby because of the physical limitations. This intensely serious look at Superman's private life may seem silly, but it reveals a changing America that expected new and more personal things from its heroes. Ten years earlier it would have been unseemly to write or discuss such matters, but social norms and mores had evolved at a rapid pace. Superman also needed to evolve and become socially relevant once again.

As American society continued to evolve, Superman stories remained defiant copies of a 1950s conservative storytelling formula. The Man of Steel's creators seemed to find a large amount of satisfaction in avoiding the discussion of social trends and cultural modifications. While Superman's storytellers sometimes incorporated minor new elements like modern clothing and newer slang, the Metropolis Marvel remained mostly unchanged throughout the 1950s and 1960s. This stubborn inability to evolve cost Superman credibility and readers. In 1961, the comic entitled *Superman* had 820,000 readers, whereas in 1969 only 511,984 people read the comic book title. Similarly, *Action Comics* had 485,000 monthly readers in 1961 but just over 377,000 by 1969. By contrast, Spider-Man, Marvel's most popular character, did not exist in 1961 but by 1969 *Amazing Spider-Man* was selling 372,352 issues a month, almost as many copies as *Action Comics*.[6] As Superman's sales were dropping, Spider-Man had gained and maintained an audience, and was becoming the cultural touchstone that Superman once had been. Spider-Man's adventures were popular on college campuses and among young hip readers, while Superman was losing fans and was becoming irrelevant. Although the Man of Steel still had a larger audience than any of the Marvel heroes, and was much better known among non-comic book readers and the American public as a whole, his popularity was eroding, and this trend would prove to be disastrous in the coming years. Something had to be done quickly before Superman lost even more fans and credibility. The Man of Steel needed to be updated, and DC had just the men for the job. Longtime *Superman* editor Mort Weisinger retired at the end of 1970 and Batman editor Julius Schwartz took over the editorial reins. Additionally Denny O'Neil, who had already revamped Batman and was revitalizing Green Lantern and Green Arrow, was now given his toughest assignment of all, that is, to make Superman relevant to a 1970s audience that no longer seemed to respect conservative institutions.

When Julius Schwartz was first offered the *Superman* editorship in 1971, he did not want the job. Schwartz told his superiors that he felt he was unable to contribute anything novel or substantial after all of the world-building of the Weisinger era. The former Batman editor finally agreed to the new assignment, but only if he could make major changes to the Man of Steel's mythology. Schwartz wanted to de-power Superman and update the hero's mythos in order to recreate the Metropolis Marvel as both more contemporary and relatable. The new *Superman* editor noted, "The way Mort [Weisinger] did Superman, he could balance the earth on one finger. But when I did Superman, he would have to use *both hands* to hold up the earth" (italics in the original).[7] One of Schwartz's first changes was to hire Denny O'Neil as the comic book's writer in an attempt to revamp the Man of Steel much as he had Batman. O'Neil also strove to create a more relevant Superman who was integrated into contemporary American society rather than judging it from a distance. The editor and writer quickly came up with a list of things that needed to be altered. Superman had to be less powerful and more human. Silly and gimmicky plot devices and overused story ideas were to be cast aside and never trotted out again. Clark Kent should be less nebbish and milquetoast, and should instead become a highly qualified and valuable professional. Lastly, Superman and Clark must look and act like modern 1970s Americans, not like 1950s holdovers. Schwartz listed these changes as such, "I want to get rid of all the kryptonite. I want to get rid of all the robots that are used to get him out of situations. And I'm sick and tired of that stupid suit that Clark Kent wears all the time. I want to give him more up-to-date clothes. And maybe the more important thing I want to do is take him out of the *Daily Planet* and put him into television."[8] By the beginning of 1971, Schwartz and O'Neil were in place and Superman was about to get a much-needed revamp.

Enter Sandman

Denny O'Neil took over the Man of Steel's writing duties in *Superman* #233 (January 1971) in a tale titled "Superman Breaks Loose." The opening page promises "A Return to Greatness!" and "An old majesty... in a stunning new tale of thrills, tragedy—and heroism."[9] The story begins with a scientific accident that turns all of the green kryptonite on Earth into lead. As Superman's supporting cast discusses the destruction of one of Superman's greatest weaknesses, readers are introduced to Morgan Edge, a media mogul who now owns the *Daily Planet* newspaper for which Clark Kent has worked for years. Edge quickly assigns Clark to television reporter duties, and before the issue's end, Kent will become a full-time television newscaster. During the course of the story, Superman prevents several criminals from stealing a rocket and manages to prove that all of the Earth's kryptonite has been destroyed by eating a piece of iron that once was the radioactive green rock. The issue ends with a sand creature forming in the desert and taking on Superman's shape. The narration creates an ominous tone as the sandman rises from the ground, walking across the barren wasteland. The description reads, "... a blazing sun beats upon the desert... upon a figure in the sand... and then, it stirs... ever so slowly... It is a thing created from soil and rock and a burst of raw energy... cast in the mold of Superman... and it lives! Like some nightmare creature, it plods toward the distant mountains...and toward the villages and towns and cities beyond... moving slowly, relentlessly to a terrible destiny."[10] Denny O'Neil had created a creature that was supposed to challenge Superman and help the Man of Steel adjust in order to better represent 1970s America. It was unclear if this sandman would succeed where so many others had failed, though, and if the long-static Man of Steel was even capable of making a change.

In Denny O'Neil's first issue of Superman, the writer quickly eliminates several tropes that had been a part of the Man of Steel's mythology for decades. Kryptonite is destroyed within the story's first four pages, although the glowing substance had menaced Superman for decades. As Schwartz also wished, Clark Kent switches jobs and diversifies his wardrobe in an attempt to appear modern and relatable. The most important long-term change is that in future issues it will be revealed that the mysterious sandman is a dark version of Superman from another dimension who is stealing the Man of Steel's powers. Eventually, the sand creature will drain off one-third of the Man of Tomorrow's superpowers and will leave Superman closer to the hero's Golden Age roots. O'Neil's sandman storyline began the process of rethinking the concept of Superman for a different generation, and would seem to be the beginning of a new era for the Man of Steel. This was not to be the case, though. O'Neil's run ended after only nine issues, with the writer reportedly unable to connect artistically with Superman in any successful way. O'Neil later noted that, at the time, he had not been enjoying writing Superman and had asked to be removed from the assignment.[11] Schwartz obliged and in the issue following O'Neil's departure, Superman returned to his previous power level as if nothing had happened. Although one-third of Superman's power had been stolen just thirty days before, by October 1971 Superman was the same old Man of Steel, just better dressed and with a new occupation. New writer Cary Bates took over with *Superman* #243 and created stories that focused on a larger-than-life and conservative Man of Steel. Superman had battled change and the Man of Steel won. Schwartz and O'Neil had attempted to make Superman less powerful and more relevant, and seemingly had failed on both accounts. There were other creators working on the Man of Steel, but they also seemed to be creating rehashed versions of old Superman stories. One of the greatest comic book creators of all time was writing a Superman spinoff, and he was having just as much trouble as other writers pulling Superman from the past into the 1970s.

In October 1970, longtime Marvel artist Jack Kirby began working for DC Comics and started writing *Superman's Pal Jimmy Olsen*. Kirby, who had become known as the "King," had worked with Stan Lee at Marvel Comics to construct many of the publisher's popular heroes, and with Joe Simon Kirby had created Captain America in the 1940s. It would not be an overstatement, and might well be a gross understatement, to claim that Jack Kirby is one of the most important comic book professionals in the industry's history. Kirby reportedly had experienced creative differences with Lee at Marvel, and came to DC looking for a fresh start and more artistic control. Comic book lore states that the King took control of the third tier Jimmy Olsen title because the book did not have a creative team, and he did not want to be responsible for getting artists and writers fired. Kirby transformed *Jimmy Olsen* stories into an odd mishmash of staple comic book elements that included World War II-era kid gangs, space aliens, gangsters, celebrities, monsters, scientists, and just bizarre storylines. Much of Kirby's *Jimmy Olsen* work was an eccentric retelling of old 1940s- and 1950s-style stories with a few contemporary elements thrown in for good measure. While Kirby changed the tone of Jimmy Olsen's comic book, he did not update the Man of Steel, and instead often included minor passages that display Superman as being out of touch. An example of this is *Superman's Pal Jimmy Olsen* #144 (December 1971), in which Superman goes to a dance club and one of the establishment's patrons makes fun of the Metropolis Marvel by offering, "Look at poor Superman! As a charter member of the establishment, he's on the defensive here."[12] In Kirby's stories (and most others after the Denny O'Neil effort), Superman was not hip or relatable, but rather he was the same dull dependable figure that he had been for over two decades. Kirby could create a World War II icon, fashion a large portion of the Marvel universe, and shape comic book stories for a generation, but even he was unable to make Superman relevant in the 1970s.

Questioning Superman

DC creators and editors fashioned several very good Superman stories during the first half of the 1970s. The tales sometimes included fascinating plotlines and villains that kept readers turning the pages. Few of these tales, however, showcased Superman as anything more than the big blue Boy Scout that many Americans identified him as. The Man of Steel's public image prevented DC from modernizing the character and this was quickly making Superman archaic. Even worse, some 1970s stories were beginning to question why Superman even existed. In *Superman* #247 (January 1972), writer Elliot S! Maggin (punctuated correctly) asked both the Man of Steel and readers, "Must There Be a Superman?" In the story, the almost godlike Guardians of the Universe, who created the Green Lantern Corps and work to safeguard the universe, attempt to cause Superman to doubt his role as Earth's caretaker and protector. The issue opens with the Man of Steel assisting the Guardians by helping to avert an intergalactic natural disaster. When Superman is taken to the Guardians' home planet, Oa, these *über*powerful little blue men decide "to implant in his subconscious the notion that his influence on Earth is interfering with human progress."[13] The Guardians mention to the Man of Tomorrow that he is harming "... human social growth" and that his "... presence on Earth directly contributes to the terrans' cultural lag!"[14] As Superman leaves, the Guardians reflect, "Our plan is progressing! His behavior-pattern indicates that our planted idea is beginning to grow in his mind. He and his adopted planet will soon be the better for it."[15] A confused Man of Steel arrives back at home and reflects, "For years I've been playing big brother to the human race! Have I been wrong? Are they depending on me too much... too often?"[16] Upon returning to Earth, Superman stops in California to break up an altercation between a landowner and a young Mexican migrant worker. A group of immigrants calls on the Metropolis Marvel to solve their problems and the text box reads, "... and if you rebuilt every ghetto and arrested every slumlord? What then, Superman?"[17] The Man of Steel then yells at the local populace, "... And what I'm going to do is Nothing! Nothing At All! Whatever help you claim you need—must come from yourselves..."[18] Just then an earthquake strikes and Superman not only moderates the natural disaster but also rebuilds the village's houses. The Man of Steel lectures the townspeople, "Let's get something straight! Sure—I rebuilt your homes, but that was because an earthquake is something you can't handle—something you can't safeguard yourself against—but you must not count on a Superman to patch up your lives every time you have a crisis or disaster..." He later adds, "You don't need a Superman! What you really need is a super-will to be guardians of your own destiny! Now

I have work to do..."[19] The Man of Steel then flies away in order to save a "pleasure cruiser endangered by a water spout..." The story ends as the Guardians of the Universe observe Superman on a monitor and reflect, "Kal-El is troubled somewhat by an idea that never crossed his mind before—the fact that people of Earth must progress unaided by outsiders from other worlds... Then our task is done! We must let time take its course!"[20]

"Must There Be a Superman?" is a peculiar story that questions the Man of Steel's relevance and denies Superman's Great Depression roots, while pushing the Metropolis Marvel down a path towards extreme social conservatism, and creating the oxymoronic idea of a libertarian superhero. This serves in contrast to Superman's origins as a Great Depression hero. Jerry Siegel and Joe Shuster created Superman in 1938 to battle slumlords and crooked politicians, and help those members of society who could not defend themselves. The children of immigrants fashioned the Man of Steel to help the very types of people that he now lectures about self-sufficiency in this story. This comic's narrative suggests that Superman is often a hindrance and liability, and he should allow people to handle their own problems, in a philosophy that seems akin to Ayn Rand's writings. This issue is groundbreaking in its attempt to examine Superman's purpose, but it deviates greatly from the Man of Steel's accepted position, and seems to declare superheroes to be misguided and irrelevant. Just a few months before, Denny O'Neil's Superman stories attempted to make the Man of Steel more contemporary and relevant; now Elliot S! Maggin proclaims the Man of Steel to be almost obsolete. Superman had become so old-fashioned and unchangeable that some of his own writers no longer believed in him. Maggin claimed that this story encapsulated the themes and ideas that he explored in the Superman stories that he created:

> It was a story in which I articulated to myself a number of the questions that eventually I tried to answer with the Superman series: What was Superman's relationship to his charges, the people of the Earth? To the authoritative functionaries of the rest of the Universe like the Guardians and, by extension, those who might be considered deities? What were the limits of Superman's responsibilities? Were there differences between the real limits of his responsibilities and his perception of those responsibilities? What role did his heritage, both on Earth and among the stars, play in the determination of his actions? What long-term effects were coming about as a result of his intercession?[21]

Maggin did address many of these topics in his tenure as *Superman* writer. Importantly, the author's work showcases a self-questioning Superman, so conservative and powerful that he is no longer relatable to the masses. While Superman had long been teetering on the edge of self-parody and inconsequence, he had now crossed the line into triviality. A self-doubting Superman was now debating whether he should help those in need and what exactly was his true purpose. The once proud Man of Steel was a beaten and battered former protector who no longer even believed in himself. Other superheroes, especially the Marvel characters, often questioned themselves and their abilities, but their writers used the heroes' foibles and feet of clay to affirm their heroicness. In this story, Superman does not overcome his reservations and misgivings, rather he gives into them. Although this change did not make Superman less old-fashioned and more readable, it did help him to better mirror an increasingly self-doubting and lost American society. The problem was that as Americans were dealing with Vietnam and the aftermath of the 1960s social upheaval, many people did not want a hesitant and distrustful Man of Steel. Superman was still overly powerful and deeply conservative, but now he also was nervous and wary, a bad combination for a society and a superhero.

The Bat Stays in the Picture

As Superman was busy questioning himself and his role in society, Batman was beginning to embrace his dark nature and battle not only standard costumed villains, but also gothic boogeymen and twisted sociopaths. Americans were attempting to adjust to their new post-1960s society and Batman warred against dark enemies that emulated the nation's fears. While Superman continued to fight thieves, evil scientists, and would-be world conquerors, the Dark Knight often fought against unsettling representations of Americans' growing anxieties. One classic example of this is Ra's al Ghul, an environmental terrorist and leader of the League of Assassins which Denny O'Neil and Neal Adams introduced in *Batman* #232 (June 1971). This first appearance begins with Ra's al Ghul (which translates as "the Demon's Head") breaking into the Batcave and revealing that he has deduced the Caped Crusader's secret identity as Bruce Wayne. Batman had just learned that someone had kidnapped Robin and now Ra's al Ghul informs the Dark Knight that his daughter, Talia, has also been abducted. (Talia al Ghul had previously flirted with and fought alongside Batman in *Detective Comics* #411 in May 1971.) Although Batman obviously does not like this new figure in his life, the two men agree to work together to find their missing loved ones. The pair travel to Calcutta and soon Batman is forced to battle and kill a leopard, take on a sniper, and test his boundaries in order to track down the Boy Wonder. In the end, it is revealed that Ra's al Ghul is responsible for the kidnappings because he wants to test Batman to see if the Dark Knight is worthy of marrying his daughter and taking over his criminal organization.[22] While not much is revealed about Ra's al Ghul's business dealings in this issue, the reader assumes he is up to no good. The issue ends with Talia taking center stage and Batman looking shocked at Ra's al Ghul's proposal.

In the next few decades Ra's al Ghul would become one of Batman's predominate foes, and a villain who defies normal stereotyping. As seen in this story, the Demon's Head is a departure from typical comic book bad guys, who predictably want to steal, create mayhem, or defeat and unmask the Dark Knight. Ra's al Ghul will cause Batman many problems over the years, but these will be new types of challenges that will often provide fresh and engaging storylines for Batman readers. The leader of the League of Assassins is not a common criminal; he has numerous needs and desires that fall outside the normal superhero spectrum of right and wrong. In future stories, it will be revealed that the Demon's Head wishes to destroy much of modern civilization and return the world to a more environmentally harmonious state. This action would undoubtedly cause the deaths of millions, if not billions, and would bring an end to life as we know it. Ra's al Ghul believes that he is committing these acts for the good of the planet and, although he is misguided, his actions do not fall into the typical comic book binary of good and bad. This more complex understanding of villainy can be seen in Ra's al Ghul's first appearance. In this story, the villain tests Batman by forcing the Dark Knight to climb mountains, battle leopards, fight henchmen, and solve the mystery of who abducted Robin. The antagonist displays within the first few pages that he is smart enough to learn Batman's secret identity and has no need to steal in the traditional sense. In the end, it is revealed that all of this is a game to prove Batman worthy of Ra's al Ghul's daughter and the family business. While many villains had tested the Dark Knight, and numerous bad guys created puzzles and games, almost all past villains were criminally insane. Most former Batman foes were presented as evil in deed and in nature. While some criminals reformed, very few had such complex motives as to make the reader question his or her understanding of right and wrong. Ra's al Ghul's first appearance lays the foundation for a complex villain who in future stories will defy comic book stereotypes. Even in this narrative, the Demon's Head is a multifaceted character who cannot successfully be categorized as villain or foe. He is an individual with an agenda that is neither good nor bad, but one that serves his purposes. This is one of the reasons that Batman looks so startled at the story's end. The Dark Knight is not accustomed to being surprised by men and their motives. Americans at this time were also just as surprised by many of the changes within society. Stories like these helped Batman to capture the tone and feeling of American society during the 1970s. Things were changing rapidly and Batman was adapting in order to keep up. Superman was not doing nearly as well.

When Relevant Goes Wrong

As Batman managed to remain in touch with American society, Superman and his supporting cast were not as fortunate. After Denny O'Neil's updating of the Man of Steel failed to take hold, Superman floundered for several years as creators attempted but were unable to successfully revitalize the Metropolis Marvel. While writers like Cary Bates and Elliot S! Maggin endeavored to make the Man of Steel fresh and exciting, Superman proved to be generally unchangeable, and the few minor alterations that were incorporated into the hero's mythology were laughably retreaded elements of established genre narratives, or were quickly abandoned (and sometimes both.) Examples of these stories and elements include the March 1972 *Superman* #249, in which our hero battles the Terra-Man. The new villain was born in the Old West era, was abducted and raised by an alien, and eventually decided to become an interstellar outlaw. Terra-Man rides a winged horse, dresses like a cowboy, uses an advanced arsenal that resembles nineteenth-century weapons, speaks in a cartoonishly clichéd western dialect, and appears to be modeled on a Clint Eastwood character from one of the actor's spaghetti westerns. In *Superman* #258 (November 1972), the Man of Steel fights the Galactic Golem, a space-based updating of a popular Jewish mythological creature. In June 1973, the Man of Tomorrow struggles against the Phantom Quarterback in *Superman* #264. In *Superman* #266 (August 1973), the hero confronts the Abominable Snowman, while in *Superman* #270 (December 1973), the Man of Steel defeats a Viking threat. As Batman was accepting society's need for a dark and serious tone that mirrored many of the real world's troubles, Superman was unable or unwilling to change. No matter what the consequences, the Man of Steel was too conservative and powerful to adjust. The Man of Steel's stories were generally new takes on old ideas even as comic book readers demanded fresh narratives.

A typical story from this era reveals a clear attempt at relevance which goes terribly wrong. In *Superman* #281 the Metropolis Marvel encounters Vartox from the planet Valeron, who has come to Earth to avenge his wife's death. Vartox's physical appearance and costume are based a Sean Connery character from the 1974 science fiction film *Zardoz*. It seems that writer Cary Bates was trying to capitalize on the film's supposed popularity and portray Superman as current and fashionable. Instead, the story reads like a mash-up of old comic book and pulp magazine clichés in a new package. In the tale, Vartox learns that a man named Frank Sykes murdered his wife's "psychic twin" on earth and this caused his life mate to die at the exact same moment because the two women were "biologically linked." At first, Superman, Vartox, and Sykes all battle one another, but eventually the Man of Steel learns of the alien's mission and helps him to capture the murderer. Sykes is extradited to Valeron, where he is tried and convicted of the women's deaths. As punishment the criminal is aged sixty years in six minutes and justice is declared to have been served. Nothing is exceptional about this story except that the tale showcases a representative Superman narrative from the period.[23] This issue of *Superman* attempted to take various social and cultural elements and mix them together to create something new. Instead of something novel, what was concocted was a hackneyed story comprising a mishmash of numerous disparate ideas. Although many comic book stories have borrowed popular culture elements from other media or society at large, and have taken old ideas and made them new, this comic book offered nothing fresh, but instead merely reheated older concepts. Unfortunately this speaks for the state of Superman stories during this time. The Man of Steel was battling villains and protecting the public, but as the years passed, he seemed to be more and more out of touch. American society was moving forward but Superman seemed to be unable to follow.

Can Lois Lane Change?

As Superman was starring in unoriginal stories in *Action Comics* and his self-titled comic book, and Jack Kirby was creating new versions of 1940s and 1950s tales, several writers were also working to make Lois Lane relevant to modern audiences in her own comic book series, *Lois Lane, Superman's Girl Friend.* DC would continue to publish issues of the magazine until October 1974, and during the late 1960s and 1970s, Lois Lane worked hard to prove herself to be both liberal and liberated. As with earlier storylines, Lois continued to assert her independence by treating Superman badly and often physically attacking him. Few could question that Lois wanted to be her own woman, but the lengths to which she went to distance herself from the Man of Steel often bordered on disturbing. While many of these actions have been discussed previously, a growing feature in Lois Lane's stories was her need to prove her progressive credentials. In a July 29, 1972 newspaper article, *The Michigan Daily* writer Diane Levick noted that Lois was trying too hard to act like the liberated woman that she was not, calling Ms. Lane "the world's most superficial feminist."[24] Examples of Lois's new forced liberal outlook abound, including *Lois Lane* #110 (May 1971), in which she adopts a Native American baby and faces both Caucasian and Native American prejudice. In April 1972's *Lois Lane* #123, Lois decides to change jobs in order to better fight for social justice. Ms. Lane stops being a *Daily Planet* staff reporter and instead becomes a freelance journalist. Regarding the decision, Lois notes, "No one will tell me what to write about—I pick my own stories... I have a responsibility to [the] people! There's far too much injustice all around to be ignored any longer!"[25] In *Lois Lane* #124-126 (July-September 1972), DC editors included a special section to answers letters regarding Lois's new, more feminist image. Interestingly, an unknown writer using the pseudonym "Alexander the Great" edited the letter column and often blasted readers who thought that feminism was a good idea. Like most things connected to Superman, *Lois Lane* writers and editors seemed to embrace older, more conservative values, even if in a sarcastic manner. One answer to a fan's letter in *Lois Lane* #125 highlights this point. In that letter page Alexander the Great replies, "There is only one way to do things, and that's the man's way. Can you imagine women in key roles of history? If it had been a woman instead of Moses, we'd have ten THOUSAND Commandments, instead of ten. And the Alamo? It would've fallen in ten minutes! "Florence of Arabia" would never have made it, and "Georgia" Washington would've drowned in the Delaware River. How can any girl in her right mind refute what I've made plain?? Forget Women's Lib. If we gave them the world, they'd ruin it!"[26]

Undoubtedly the strangest Lois Lane story of the 1970s is contained in *Superman's Girl Friend Lois Lane* #106 (November 1970). The tale, entitled "I Am Curious (Black)!" has Lois transforming into a black women in order to understand African-Americans' problems. The title of the story is a homage to the 1960s Swedish films *I Am Curious (Yellow)* and *I Am Curious (Blue)*, which address such topics as class, race, and gender in Swedish society. The comic book story seems to have more in common with the 1961 nonfiction book *Black Like Me*, in which the white author, John Howard Griffin, travels the southern United States passing as a black man. In this narrative, Superman uses a Kryptonian device to turn Lois Lane into a black woman for twenty-four hours, so that the formerly white reporter can better understand what life is like for an African-American person living in the United States. Before her transformation, Lois could not get a single black person to talk to her, and one African-American man makes a speech in which he exclaims, "Look at her, brothers and sisters! She's young and sweet and pretty! But never forget... she's whitey! She'll let us shine her shoes and sweep her floors! And baby-sit her kids! But she doesn't want to let our kids into her lily-white schools! It's okay with her if we leave these rat-infested slums! If we don't move next door to her! That's why she's our enemy!" After hearing this, Lois thinks, "He's wrong about me… but right about so many others!"[27] Subsequently, Lois temporarily becomes black; she experiences several small acts of racism that help her to understand how difficult life must be for actual African-Americans. A familiar cab driver will not pick her up and white people stare at her on the subway. A kindly black woman invites Lois into her home and offers the newly African-American reporter hospitality even though the apartment is falling apart and infested with rats. The woman's positive attitude prompts Lois to reflect later, "She lives in misery… yet asks if she can help me!"[28] Lois then encounters the man from before who called her the enemy, and watches as mobsters shoot him as he tries to stop drug dealing from ruining the neighborhood. Upon arriving at the hospital, Lois is amazed to discover that she and her former enemy have the same blood type and are very closely related under their skins. She provides the blood for a transfusion and then asks Superman the only question that matters at a time like this, "Suppose I couldn't change back? Would you marry me? Even if I'm black? An outsider in a white man's world?"[29] The Man of Steel replies, "You ask that of me… Superman? An alien from Krypton… another planet? A universal outsider? I don't even have human skin! It's tougher than steel!"[30] Before they can finish the argument, Lois Lane transforms back into her naturally white self and the wounded patient awakens. Lois is frightened that the young man will abhor her but Superman opines, "If he still hates you… with your blood in his veins… there may never be peace in this world!" The story ends with a page composed of seven silent panels in which the injured man realizes what Lois has done, his expressions changes from horror to happiness, and he finally takes her hand into his.[31]

Robert Kanigher almost certainly wrote "I Am Curious (Black)!" with the intention of raising social consciousness and creating a more unified, understanding, and harmonious society. The story did not fulfill these lofty goals; rather the narrative is fairly juvenile, even by the comic book standards of the day. Lois Lane's attempts to prove her liberal credentials by sympathizing with Metropolis' African-American population often seem condescending and the story's ending wraps things up much too neatly. Superman's brief portrayal highlights perfectly the Man of Steel's growing irrelevance during the 1970s, and makes it easy to see why many comic books readers thought the Metropolis Marvel to be out of touch with their wants and needs. In the story, Superman changes Lois into a black woman and does not intervene again until he believes she is in danger, even as he does nothing while another man is shot nearby. Notice that Superman does not support any of the people whom Lois encounters and does not attempt to stop the young man from being shot, but rather only endeavors to help his "girlfriend." Superman then argues with Lois that he is the ultimate outsider who is not accepted by anyone throughout the universe. This declaration seems preposterous coming from one of the very symbols of American cultural hegemony, who is beloved in both the real and numerous fictional universes. The very action of Superman purporting to be a misunderstood outcast reveals how irrelevant the character had become. Superman had once been an outsider who terrified many members of the general public, but those days were long past. That Superman lived in a world that did not understand him, and yet he continued to labor to make street-level changes. By contrast, in the early and mid-1970s Superman paid lip service to producing change, but in reality was a hero who had no stomach for new social ideas or practices. This Superman was still a keeper of the status quo, the ultimate insider who could not and would not break his ties to the governing powers. As society began to fear political, business, and social leaders more and more, Superman was hamstrung by the powerful connections that had once proven to be extremely beneficial. During the early part of the 1970s, Superman was unable to change because, by his very nature, he was a guardian of peace and normality, two of the biggest opponents of transformation. Comic book creators tried to alter Superman, but always failed, because the Man of Steel was a caretaker of the state and those in power, and there was little that could be done to break these ties.

Things Fall Apart

By the end of 1975, the United States was reeling from an abundance of political, economic, and social misfortunes. In August 1974, President Richard Nixon resigned in the aftermath of the Watergate scandal, which had rocked the nation for over a year. This, added to the recently ended Vietnam conflict, the economic recession, and the unelected President Gerald Ford, left many Americans feeling a myriad of negative emotions, including apathy and discontent. Many believed that the nation had lost its way and it was unclear what could and should be done. When leaders can be assassinated, presidents lie, tens of thousands die in a seemingly pointless conflict, inflation runs rampant, and life appears to worsen daily, then what could the average American believe in? The decade had started with many Americans trying to adjust to a new post-1960s society, and by the midpoint of the decade, the country seemed to be losing all sense of balance and control. Those who turned to comic book superheroes for answers received a mixed bag at best. Superman remained the same ultrapowerful Boy Scout who championed the status quo and paid lip service to progressive ideas, while his actions perpetuated the existing state of affairs. Many had tried to change the Man of Steel, but none had succeeded. Batman's creators, on the other hand, were continuing to explore the character's dark side while channeling much of the ever-present fear and paranoia that seemed to run rampant throughout society. In September 1973's *Batman* #251, Denny O'Neil pens an adventure in which the Caped Crusader battles his archnemesis the Joker. In this story, and in other later 1970s tales, the Clown Prince of Crime has turned from a ridiculous clown into a cold-blooded killer who murders for both profit and sport.[32] *Batman* #255 (March 1974) features a story entitled "Moon of the Wolf," in which the Dark Knight fights an evil-scientist-controlled werewolf. While both of these characters are comic book staples, the tone of the story pushes the reader towards fear and dread. The tale's second page opens with a dialogue box that highlights the story's, and the nation's, dark attitude, "Tis said that it takes a special kind of talent to survive in your modern city... a mixture of sheer nerve, animal cunning, and a casual acceptance of the otherwise unbelievable."[33] Denny O'Neil's "Catwoman's Circus Caper" (Batman #256, June 1974) ends with Batman successfully capturing his feline adversary, but lamenting that his life never seems to change for the better.[34] These tales, showcasing the Caped Crusader's existential angst, stand in contrast to many past stories and fit perfectly with the society's new outlook. Like most Americans, Batman also seemed to be trapped in a dark place, but unlike many peoples, at least the Dark Knight's pain and torment was entertaining.

Possibly the comic book creation that best points out the nature of Batman stories during the early to mid-1970s is Man-Bat. The new character, which debuted in *Detective Comics* #400 (June 1970), is a horrific twisted mirror of Batman's hopes and ideals born into an America that is coming to grips with a multitude of horrors. Man-Bat is the scientist Kirk Langstrom who, through a series of experiments, becomes a human-sized bat. After transforming into Man-Bat, Langstrom loses control of his faculties and goes on a rampage before eventually battling Batman. What separates Man-Bat from many comic book characters is his loneliness, sadness, and the internal horror at what he has become. Rarely has a comic book hero/villain displayed such a palpable degree of self-loathing and derision. As Langstrom transforms into Man-Bat, the scientist fights against what he has become and desperately tries to keep a grasp on his humanity. Langstrom is so horrified by his new identity that he attempts to hide from those around him and endeavors to create an antidote to revert to what he once was. Man-Bat is the perfect symbol for the first half of the 1970s in Batman comics and, to a large extent, American society. The monstrous creature is neither hero nor villain but rather a character who defies traditional labels. He is a sad and lonely being who once was something far greater, but now only hopes to return to his past glory. Man-Bat is the grotesque shell of the human being he once was. Kirk Langstrom is tortured by the knowledge that he has done this to himself and is alone responsible for what he has become.[35] Numerous U.S. citizens could undoubtedly understand Man-Bat's feelings of terror and horror regarding his transformation. At the midpoint of the 1970s many Americans tried desperately to understand what they had become while clinging to what they once had been. The Vietnam conflict was over, the Watergate Scandal had passed, and the nation had to once again transform to survive. A lonesome and wounded Man-Bat modeled the floundering country, which in turn fills the stories with both interest and horror. Many Americans were unhappy with their nation's transformation and looked on with revulsion as their lives continued to grow more and more grotesque. As Batman battled against nighttime terrors, most Americans understood all too well what it was like to be confused and afraid.

Conclusion

The first half of the 1970s was a period of transition and a time to face new challenges and combat unforeseen problems. The 1960s were over and Americans had to reconstruct their society while facing the social pressures of war, economic downturn and political scandal. These trials and tribulations pushed citizens towards a darker place and fostered rapid changes, both positive and negative. Like many of their fellow Americans, Superman and Batman approached these social changes in vastly different ways. Superman, like numerous older and more conservative Americans, generally resisted change and chose to instead embrace traditional values and understandings. While this was feasible during the 1950s and even the 1960s, it became less and less acceptable as time passed. Even when the Man of Steel eventually tried to evolve, he was fundamentally unable to transform from his highly conservative persona. He, like many citizens, faced a rapidly changing world for which he was unprepared and innately unable to cope. Batman, on the other hand, proved to be much more resourceful and adaptable. The Caped Crusader embraced his darker side and celebrated a new, more serious tone that reflected what many Americans were feeling and thinking. While Superman could do little to ingratiate himself with comic book readers, Batman writers seemed to understand the nation's direction and consistently adjusted their stories accordingly. The Man of Steel and the Dark

Knight showcase American society's changes during the first half of the 1970s. They display how two very different heroes dealt with the decade's challenges. One hero was wedded to the past and unable to allow himself to change, while another seemed to happily follow the social currents wherever they might lead. Once again the two heroes were casting a mirror on a lost and often frightened America, a notion that promised to only intensify during the latter half of the decade.

Notes

1 "Yogi Berra Quotes." *Yogi-isms.* Accessed on June 12, 2012. http://www.umpirebob.com/DATA/yogiisms.htm.

2 "The Evolution of Batman." June 21, 2007. *AMC Blog*. Accessed June 18, 2012. http://blogs.amctv.com/movie-blog/2007/06/the-evolution-o.php.

3 Denny O'Neil and Neal Adams. "The Secret of the Waiting Graves." *Detective Comics* #395 (New York: DC Comics, January 1970).

4 Larry Niven. "Man of Steel, Woman of Kleenex." Accessed on June 19, 2012. http://www.rawbw.com/~svw/superman.html#Reprinted.

5 Niven. "Man of Steel."

6 "1969 Comic Book Sales Figures." Accessed June 17, 2012. http://www.comichron.com/yearlycomicssales/1960s/1969.html.

7 Les Daniels. *Superman: The Complete History* (San Francisco, CA: Chronicle Books, 1998): 132.

8 Daniels. *Superman*: 132-133

9 Denny O'Neil and Curt Swan. "Superman Breaks Loose." *Superman* #233 in *DC Comics Classics Library, Superman: Kryptonite Nevermore* (New York: DC Comics, 2009): 10.

10 O'Neil and Swan. *DC Comics Classics*: 24.

11 Denny O'Neil and Ed Gross. "Exclusive Interview: Denny O'Neil on Humanizing Superman." January 26, 2009. *ComicBookMovie.com*. Accessed on May 24, 2012. http://www.comicbookmovie.com/fansites/VoicesFromKrypton/news/?a=6067.

12 Jack Kirby. "A Bug Thing in a Deep Scottish Lake." *Superman's Pal Jimmy Olsen* #144 (New York: DC Comics, December 1971): 7.

13 Elliot S! Maggin and Curt Swan. "Must There Be A Superman?" *Superman* #247 in *The Greatest Superman Stories Ever Told* (New York: DC Comics, 1987): 260.

14 Maggin and Swan. *The Greatest*: 260-261.

15 Maggin and Swan. *The Greatest*: 263.

16 Maggin and Swan. *The Greatest*.

17 Maggin and Swan. *The Greatest*: 267.

18 Maggin and Swan. *The Greatest*.

19 Maggin and Swan. *The Greatest*: 270.

20 Maggin and Swan. *The Greatest*: 271.

21 Elliot S! Maggin. "Must There Be A Superman?" *Superman Through the Ages*. Accessed July 27, 2012. http://supermanthrutheages.com/esm/must.php.

22 Denny O'Neil and Neal Adams. "Daughter of the Demon." *Batman* #232 (New York: DC Comics, June 1971).

23 Cary Bates and Nick Cardy. "Mystery Mission to Metropolis." *Superman* #281 (New York: DC Comics, November 1974.)

24 Diane Levick. "The 'Liberation' of Lois Lane." *The Michigan Daily*. July 29, 1972. *Google News*. Accessed August 21, 2012. http://news.google.com/

25 Cary Bates and Bob Oksner. "The Ten Deadly Visions of the 100." *Superman's Girl Friend Lois Lane* # 123 (New York: DC Comics, June 1972): 3.

26 Letter Column. *Superman's Girl Friend Lois Lane* #125 (New York: DC Comics, August 1972).

27 Robert Kanigher and Curt Swan. "I Am Curious (Black)!" *Superman's Girl Friend Lois Lane* #106 (New York: DC Comics, November 1970): 4.

28 Kanigher and Swan. *Superman's Girl Friend*:, 8.

29 Kanigher and Swan. *Superman's Girl Friend*: 12.

30 Kanigher and Swan. *Superman's Girl Friend*: 12-13.

31 Kanigher and Swan. *Superman's Girl Friend*: 13-14.

32 Denny O'Neil and Neal Adams. "The Joker's Five-Way Revenge." *Batman* #251 (New York: DC Comics, September 1973.)

33 Len Wein and Neal Adams. "Moon of the Wolf." *Batman* #255 (New York: DC Comics, March 1974): 2.

34 Denny O'Neil and Irv Novick. "Catwoman's Circus Caper!" *Batman* #256 (New York: DC Comics, October 1974).

35 Frank Robbins and Neal Adams. "Challenge of the Man-Bat." *Detective Comics* #400 (New York: DC Comics, June 1970).

CHAPTER 4

Where Do We Go From Here? 1975–1979

The second half of the 1970s began very differently than the first half had. While 1970 had commenced with trepidation and fear, many Americans believed that the nation could adjust to the 1960s political and social changes and create a better society. The events during the latter years of that decade had soured numerous citizens on the hopes and dreams that had once flourished, but a number of people still trusted that American exceptionalism would ensure the nation's future prosperity. By January 1976, fewer Americans seemed to hope that the future could be as good as the past. The memory of the recently ended Vietnam conflict continued to hang over the country like a dense, dark fog. The Watergate scandal had sapped many Americans' faith and trust in government, and a substantial number of citizens believed President Gerald Ford to be an ineffectual and embarrassing leader. On top of this, the country was in an economic downturn, an energy crisis was brewing, crime appeared to be rampant, and once-great cities seemed to be becoming crumbling, lawless urban wastelands. Hope was disappearing and in its place were only fear and despair. The previously prosperous nation was facing a series of economic, political, and social crises unlike any that had been seen since the Great Depression. Much like the late 1930s, American society needed heroes, and in times past Superman and Batman had stepped forward to help the nation in its hour of need. Things had changed, though, and it seemed as if the super duo no longer had the ability to comfort and inspire. During the intervening years, Superman had become an overly powerful self-important icon who now acted morally and culturally superior to those he protected. The Man of Steel was no longer a servant of the people, but rather an agent of the state who rarely missed an opportunity to correct and train those around him. Batman had been able to morph and change during the 1960s and early 1970s to better meet society's new needs and desires. During the latter 1970s, the Dark Knight also began to succumb to the growing wave of inertia and apathy that was overtaking many of the citizens of the United States. In many of his adventures, the Dark Knight appeared to be merely going through the motions, with his heart no longer in his former all-consuming quest. This mirrored Superman's well-over-a-decade-long actions and also emulated the greater struggle inherent in latter 1970s society. From 1976 to 1979 Americans needed their heroes to guide and entertain them. Unfortunately Superman and Batman were just as lost and apathetic as everyone else.

Fig. 0.5
Superman in the 1970s.
Artist: Eduardo Barretto.
™ and © DC Comics
Used by permission.

Along Came a Spider

Most Americans remember 1976 as the year of the bicentennial celebration. It was the year that a nation in turmoil, worried about the present and the future, turned its collective eyes towards the past. Millions of Americans decided to celebrate the nation's history and remember the country's founding two hundred years earlier. Americans cloaked themselves in all things red, white, and blue, and did their best to remain positive as unrelenting problems mounted. Superman, who continued to revel in his bloated powerfulness and authoritarian nature, also turned towards a feel-good spectacle that distracted readers from focusing on their everyday existence. DC and Marvel Comics editors had agreed to coproduce a special comic book story in which Superman and Spider-Man share an adventure for the first time. To non-comic-book fans this may sound like a rather mundane and easily conceived idea, because putting Marvel's most popular character in the same story as DC's best-selling and most iconic superhero would surely garner exceptional sales. Comic book readers understood that this story created a superhero détente that briefly thawed a funny-book cold war that had been building since the early 1960s. By publishing this story, DC was collaborating with an arch-rival that, only a few years before, this the elder company's employees had regarded as inferior, amateurish, and unprofessional. Possibly more important, by starring with Spider-Man in this story, Superman was admitting that the wall-crawler was his colleague and acknowledging Spidey's superheroing efforts. This displays how quickly Spider-Man had risen and how far Superman had fallen in the last decade. Ten years before, it would have been impossible to imagine such a story, because Superman would never have shared the page with the young upstart. By 1976, the Man of Steel needed a sales boost, though, and the Web Head benefited from the gravitas of fighting alongside a cultural icon. Like a meeting between old royalty and new money, the pairing was often uncomfortable and produced mixed results, but it did profit both heroes. Times were changing and a Superman in decline was looking for any help that he could find. Although many Americans did not want to think about their country in those terms, most could empathize.

Superman vs The Amazing Spider-Man #1 features a ninety-six-page story called "The Battle of the Century," and although the title is typical comic book hyperbole, the tale certainly captured the interest of numerous readers. The narrative is designed around a villain-induced plot that initially provokes Superman and Spider-Man to fight each other and then team up to stop the new Lex Luthor-Doctor Octopus partnership from destroying the world. As expected, the story ends with the two heroes capturing the bad guys and foiling the evil plot. There are several story scenes that illustrate Superman's mid-1970s characteristics and relatability problems. The most telling of these is the plot beat in which the two heroes first meet and square off. For this battle Lex Luthor and Doctor Octopus have covered Spider-Man in red sun radiation, which weakens the Man of Steel and almost physically evens the contest. As Spider-Man hits Superman, the webslinger taunts the Man of Steel and at one point opines, "Well, I've got a newsflash for you, Supes! You're not half so tough as you think you are!"[1] The young upstart not only physically beats the veteran comic book icon but also verbally assaults his elder. Metatextually this can be read as Spider-Man asserting his growing real-world popularity and sales power inside his and Superman's fictional realities. Superman is shocked by this revelation and cannot believe that that is happening. Eventually, though, Spider-Man's newfound red-sun-induced power fades and the wall-crawler's blows have no effect on the Man of Steel. Superman stands silently and unemotionally as Spider-Man strikes him repeatedly, the Man of Tomorrow apparently not even feeling the haymakers. The sequence ends with Spider-Man halting the fight because he has broken both of his hands punching the impervious Man of Steel.[2] Although Superman wins this fictional battle by displaying his extreme powerfulness, at the same time he reveals how he is growing out of touch with American society. This narrative's Spider-Man is cocky, playful, fun, humorous, flawed, and very relatable. He is a superhero with human frailties, who is not so powerful that he has lost his humanity. In contrast, Superman often seems devoid of weakness or emotion. He is so accustomed to being supremely powerful that he views it as his birthright. Superman is efficient, hard-working, calm, stoic, and frankly dull. The Man of Steel had always been an alien but in his early years was the most human of characters. By forcing Superman to appear next to Spider-Man, the writers and artists revealed the Man of Steel's most deep-seated flaw, the notion that he seemingly had no flaws. Spider-Man was a wise-cracking youngster who was a failure at most things he tried, but he also forced readers to identify with and root for him. Superman was an efficient crime-fighting machine who inspired little emotion, even among his fans. Spider-Man was an everyman and Superman almost a deity, a problem that Superman editors and writers had tried to correct for years but to no avail. In the story, Superman and Spider-Man walked away from "The Battle of the Century" as friends, but in the real world Spider-Man was faring much better. Ironically Superman was losing the battle of public opinion because he was much too powerful and not human enough, the very qualities that helped him defeat fictional criminals. Much like the United States, Superman needed to change and to change, soon.

As Superman was battling and befriending Spider-Man, Batman was continuing his grim and gritty ways. The Dark Knight was struggling against a bleak and decaying urban landscape that endangered not only his physical presence but also his mental and emotional wellbeing. The city continuously produced new and more dangerous menaces that threatened the Caped Crusader's mind, body, and soul. While Superman stood above the fray almost casually and omnipotently, the non-superpowered Batman descended monthly into filth and madness in order to wage his personal war against lawlessness. Crime had become front-page news in many places in the United States, as Americans worried that criminals were controlling the streets and the country was no longer safe for average citizens. Reports of mass murderers, serial rapists, muggers, and numerous other criminal types filled the nation's collective consciousness, and fueled the already growing fear and paranoia. An America awash in post-Vietnam and post-Watergate grief turned its hardened gaze to its seemingly unsafe streets and its apparently grotesque and out of control cities. A society in mourning for the placid and secure 1950s metamorphosed its crime-ridden cities into the symbol of the nation's decay. By 1977, once-great metropolises like New York City seemed replete with crime, corruption, and unrest. When the city teetered on the edge of bankruptcy in 1975 and a massive electrical power outage caused a blackout, combined with the Son of Sam's killing spree in 1977, hope seemed lost. Around this same time, many Midwestern and East Coast cities lost much of their manufacturing base, which initiated a chain reaction that resulted in higher unemployment, fewer city services, increased crime, and a deteriorating infrastructure. As the U.S. and its cities battled against what often seemed to be insurmountable odds, Batman followed these social cues and redoubled his efforts. The costumed hero fought for his city's survival by warring against frightening criminals and terrifying villains. The Caped Crusader reflected the fear that many Americans increasingly felt in their daily lives. As American society became darker and more horrifying, so did the Dark Knight's adventures. Batman was intensifying his anticrime campaign as Americans needed it the most.

One of the seminal Batman storylines of this period is Steve Englehart's eight-issue run in *Detective Comics* #469-476 (May 1977-April 1978). In this narrative, the author's intent was to make Batman more palatable to adult readers by introducing a new love interest, Silver St. Cloud, rebranding the Joker as the Dark Knight's archnemesis and emphasizing "... the dark, pulp roots of the character."[3] One the new characters whom Englehart created for these stories is a corrupt politician/underworld boss named Rupert Thorne. Councilman Thorne, and other members of the Gotham City Council, declare the Dark Knight a vigilante and issue a cease and desist order again Batman in an attempt to legally prevent the superhero from fighting crime. Boss Thorne is involved in numerous illegal activities and wishes to stop Batman from interfering with his money-making operations. Initially, Thorne is blackmailed by the radioactive villain, Dr. Phosphorus, but the tainted politician proves to be just as malicious and unlawful after the bad doctor is captured and incarcerated. Thorne unsuccessfully runs for mayor of Gotham City and tries to learn Batman's secret identity by bidding for the information in a villain-run auction, but by story's end, the civil servant confesses his crimes and is sent to prison. It is telling that this powerful new villain is a corrupt politician who uses both legal and illegal methods to fight the Dark Knight. Richard Nixon's involvement in the Watergate scandal had psychologically wounded many members of American society. Numerous citizens were shocked to learn that a sitting U.S. president could be tangled up in the illegal activities of which Richard Nixon was accused. Although Nixon was never convicted of any criminal wrongdoing, he did destroy many Americans' faith and trust in their political representatives. This distrust of politicians is evident in the Boss Thorne character. As Americans became more wary of corrupt politicians the creators added examples of crooked politicos to the Dark Knight's stable of villains. Batman was keeping up with the times, and, unfortunately a growing number of Americans had lost faith in the political system.

The main thread that runs through Steve Englehart's Batman stories is the notion of using the law to commit immoral acts or to aid evildoers. Past villains generally perpetrated criminal acts in a straightforward manner that created a black-and-white worldview. Good guys produced good actions and bad guys violated legal codes. Many of Englehart's stories concentrate on the difference between illegal and immoral, and what happens when villains devise nefarious yet legal schemes. In these tales, the line between right and wrong is blurred and the law is revealed to be a loophole-ridden code that can be abused without being broken. All of the stories feature the aforementioned bad politician, Rupert Thorne. During one tale, the villain, Hugo Strange, attempts to hold an auction in order to reveal the Caped Crusader's secret identity, and in another adventure, even Batman lies to avoid a subpoena that he does not wish to acknowledge. One of the best-known of Englehart's Batman stories is a two-part tale from *Detective Comics* #475 and #476 respectively titled "The Laughing Fish" and "The Sign of the Joker." In this story, the Joker tries to make himself wealthy in a devious but legal manner. The Clown Prince of Crime invents a chemical concoction that changes a fish's appearance, giving it a smile that resembles the Joker's. The Harlequin of Hate then attempts to copyright the fish's new smiley manifestation so that he will receive a percentage of each seafood purchase. When a bureaucrat informs the Joker that it is impossible to copyright a natural resource, the villain returns to his criminal ways and promises to kill government officials until his copyright application is successfully processed. While the Joker has no inclination to cease his violent criminal outlook, he takes delight in the idea of operating within the law to produce negative consequences. In the villain's mind, it is just as much fun to use the law to help himself and harm others as it is to commit crimes. While the law does not allow the Clown Prince of Crime to implement his scheme, it does provide numerous loopholes that both villain and hero alike utilize throughout the eight issues.[4] As many real-world American citizens had lost trust in their government, Batman's fictional world was becoming more like readers' reality. The comic book definition of good was no longer synonymous with legal and bad with illegal. Batman was continuing to mirror real life within the United States and his world was becoming even darker because of it.

Supervillains

As Batman's world continued to mirror American society by embracing a darker and more jaded view of politics and the law, Superman's villains became more ferocious and terrifying. Writer Marty Pasko wanted to make the Man of Steel's enemies more dangerous in order to better threaten Superman. Where the Metropolis Marvel's rogues' gallery had once been easily defeated, now they were much more menacing. Pasko noted, "... I believed that the only problem with most of the existing villains was that they needed to be made 'bigger'—more powerful, more grandiose, more desperate—to give Supes a real challenge."[5] Pasko began this approach in *Superman* #305 (November 1976), in which the scripter brings back the original Toyman, Winslow Schott. In previous adventures, creators had portrayed the Schott Toyman as a rather mundane toy-themed villain who never proved to be a major threat. Superman always dispatched Schott easily, with little effort or fanfare. Winslow Schott retired as Toyman and became Superman's crime-fighting ally in *Action Comics* #432 (February 1974). In that issue, a new, deadlier Toyman, Jack Nimball, is introduced. The new Nimball Toyman only appears three other times before meeting his untimely demise in Pasko's *Superman* #305. In this story, Winslow Schott is convinced that Superman has destroyed many of his toys and declares revenge on the Man of Steel. One of his first acts after re-initiating his Toyman persona is to murder a sleeping Jack Nimball, the "... usurper—the pretender to my throne... the throne of the king of Superman's costumed foes!"[6] The issue includes a rather predictable battle, although Toyman has now upgraded his power considerably. At one point, the villain claims that his technology makes him Superman's physical equal. In retrospect, the most important story point, though, is that Toyman easily and nonchalantly murders two people, including an innocent victim. In the past, Toyman had been a goofy C-level character that was mostly used for comic relief and an overall sense of fun. Now Toyman was a coldblooded killer whose murders were not even a major turning point in the story, but rather minor plot elements. In simpler times, villains were easily dispatched and caused little real harm to society. In the mid-1970s, Americans had much more to fear and this becomes a large part of Superman's new existence. Toyman's transformation was just the beginning, though; there were numerous other dangerous threats for the Man of Steel to battle. A change that mirrored society's heightened disheartened and fearful state.

At the end of *Superman* #305, the Toyman converses with Bizarro and informs the imperfect Superman clone that he will turn him into a normal person if the creature will kill Superman. In that issue and the next, Bizarro goes on a rampage, destroying numerous buildings in Metropolis, and kidnaps Lois Lane because he believes that his home world, containing all of his friends and family, has been destroyed. The effects of a cosmic storm appear to have made the creature more powerful and formidable than he was in the past. Bizarro had been featured in Superman stories numerous times since the late 1950s, but the character had always served as more of a concept than a villain. Created by Lex Luthor, Bizarro is an imperfect duplicate of Superman who is the opposite of the Man of Steel in most ways. The backwards Superman uses a mixed-up sentence structure when he speaks, lives on a square-shaped planet named Htrae (Earth spelled backwards), and normally acts in a manner that makes little sense to average humans. Before this issue, Bizarro generally caused problems only because he is feeble-minded and often misunderstood. Although the issue ends with Superman showing Bizarro that Htrae has not been destroyed and getting the duplicate to leave Earth, Bizarro now has become much more frightening than before. Bizarro is still a misunderstood creature, but suddenly he is also increasingly powerful, uncontrollable, and bitter. In the past, Bizarro was a chaotic force who possessed no ill will or animosity. Now the creature seems to resent his station in life and demonstrates hostility towards the Man of Steel. Bizarro was once a curiosity, but now he is a ticking bomb who could return at any time to wreak havoc and destruction. This storyline wraps up nicely with Superman escorting Bizarro home and Toyman expressing how sorry he is for blaming the Man of Steel for his broken toys. The tale has an ominous moment in the last few panels, though, when Superman reflects on what has transpired in the tale and states, "[Toyman's] murders… Bizarro's rages…all the ingratitude… for nothing! I don't think all that's going to be easy to… accept!"[7] Superman has difficulty accepting the bitterness and harshness that has begun to fill his world and real-life American society as a whole. The Man of Steel was still ultra-powerful, highly conservative, and very domineering, but his realm of existence was becoming less and less the happy place that it once had been. Many Americans also felt like they were surrounded by powerful nemeses and unfortunately they could not dispatch them as easily as Superman could.

Just as Superman's enemies were becoming more powerful and his world much darker, the Man of Steel started to exhibit signs that he was unable to cope with his changing surroundings. The next three issues of *Superman* would showcase the Man of Tomorrow growing much more violent and aggressive, while seemingly losing control of his temper. This odd three-part story written by Gerry Conway features an impetuous Superman who seems to act on emotion instead of the calculated, dispassionate Man of Steel to which readers were undoubtedly accustomed. The tale begins with Superman declaring, "This entire plant must be destroyed—even if I have to tear it apart—brick by brick!"[8] After this, the Man of Steel briefly battles a pollution-loving mutant villain, and the story flashes back to a laborer at the factory who informs Clark Kent that several workers were developing cancer because of chemicals they worked with, and the company did nothing to prevent this. Superman tours the plant and speaks with the chemical company's president, Morton Kalmbach, who notifies the Man of Steel that he understands that some of the workers are becoming ill but that is "… a socially acceptable risk" because the company is making money and helping the American economy and society. Superman then goes berserk, yelling at the white-collar company men and demolishing the nearby equipment. The Man of Tomorrow sermonizes, "Hold it! Men are dying, Kalmbach—getting cancer from working in your vats—and you say that risk is acceptable? NO! People like you are destroying this planet, killing its people, ruining its future—and for what? Profit—Greed—And some sick illusion called 'progress'! It's going to end, Kalmbach—and it's going to end right now!"[9] Superman begins to destroy the plant, leading to the sequence that opened the story. He then flies off to a mountain top and seems to have a mental or emotional breakdown as he remembers Krypton's destruction and compares it to the problems facing Earth. The Man of Steel reflects that he cannot allow humans to destroy the world and lose another planet, and then screams to the sky, "Hear me world! I won't let you commit planetary suicide! I swear I won't let you die—I swear it!" Superman proceeds to throw or force several seamen from the deck of a supertanker into the ocean, "… gathering sailors like so many toys." The Man of Steel moralizes that these oil transport ships have been involved in three accidents in the last few years which have had or can have terrible consequences for the environment. Superman then plans, "No more! I am going to throw this baby into orbit, and then come back for all the others!"[10] A villain attacks Superman before he can complete his task, and eventually Supergirl confronts the Man of Steel and tries to change his erratic behavior.

This three-issue storyline presents Superman behaving in such an irregular and detrimental manner that it reads like a 1950s story in which some outside agent or reason is causing the Man of Steel to act this bizarrely. In the early postwar years, elements like red kryptonite or secret deals to protect the universe often forced Superman to behave strangely. These actions were always explained by story's end, though, and the Metropolis Marvel was declared to be physically and mentally sound, and to have had a good reason for conducting himself irregularly. In this case, the only explanation is that Superman became so worried that the Earth would be destroyed like his home planet of Krypton, that he would do anything to prevent this. At the end of *Superman* #309, the Man of Steel explains his actions to his cousin, Supergirl, by stating, "If I'm obsessed with Earth, it's not because of Krypton—it's because of Earth, my home. I'm not ashamed of that obsession, Supergirl ... I'm proud of it! Every man and woman on Earth should feel what I feel ..."[11] Earlier in this storyline, Supergirl had been so worried about Superman's actions that she conspired with several other Kryptonians to lie to the Man of Steel in order to facilitate his better mental health. Kryptonian psychologists advise the Maid of Might to lie to Superman and convince him that he is not from Krypton, to help him cope with his overwhelming feeling of loss regarding his dead planet, and prevent him from continuing his destructive actions. In other words, Supergirl and numerous Kryptonian experts believe that Superman is so mentally unstable and so dangerous that they must deceive him in order to help him manage his psychological issues. The other Kryptonians fear for Superman's safety and more so for the Earth's wellbeing, because Superman is placing those around him and the entire planet in jeopardy.

This Gerry Conway story is both odd and unsettling, because there is little resolution to Superman's actions and his mental breakdown. In *Superman* #307, the Man of Steel starts to destroy private property because he does not agree with the owner's business principles. He then throws several laborers off their ship and into the ocean because he wants to destroy a tanker that may one day be involved in an accident that could harm the environment. While these actions are reminiscent of the Great Depression Superman's fight against street-level evils, in which he would often harm bad guys and cause mass destruction, it seems unacceptable to this mid-1970s version of the Man of Steel. The Golden Age Superman was a rambunctious hero for a rough-and-tumble time. That Superman was a quirky and humorous force of nature that showed little respect for authority and enjoyed thumbing his nose at social conventions and legal requirements. The mid- to late-1970s Superman is a hero who has lost touch with society and is searching for his identity. He is no longer a young man who enjoys the thrill and challenge of what he does, but rather a confused and tortured middle-aged person who cannot cope with his life and the changing world around him. Superman no longer understands American society and is uncertain how he should act and what is acceptable behavior. In other words, the Man of Steel is going through a midlife crisis. Because he is

Superman, he cannot just buy leather pants or a new sports car, but rather must remake his life by literally remaking the world itself. (In this issue, Clark Kent also flirts with a much younger woman while continuing to date Lois Lane, and plays football in order to better connect with those around him.) The frightening element is that at issue's end, no one seems concerned that Superman is mentally unstable and out of control. The Man of Steel justifies his actions by stating that he acted this way because he loves the Earth so much; Supergirl finds this logic to be acceptable. The Maid of Might does not hold Superman to a higher standard, and the Man of Steel does revert back to his former self. He is still a very confused individual with almost godlike powers, but Supergirl and his colleagues seems to trust him to work out his mental and emotional issues on his own. He is Superman, and thus beyond reproach. Although he was in a state of crisis, Superman was still the greatest superhero of them all.

Superman's developing mental and emotional crisis could very easily be seen as symbolic of the United States' political, economic, and social crises of the 1970s. These societal traumas caused many of the incredibly powerful nation's citizenry to begin experiencing their own crises of identity, belief, and faith in their country. While the U.S. remained politically, economically, and militarily powerful, a substantial number of Americans no longer trusted the government, society, and those around them. Faith in the "American way of life" had been a foundational belief for most Americans, and now many were questioning the country's basic tenets and fearing both the present and the future. This Superman-in-crisis story served as a proxy for what many Americans were feeling as they were living through tumultuous times and what appeared to many to be not just an economic downturn, but a social one as well. The thought of a hero as powerful as Superman facing a psychological crisis so severe that he is no longer certain what to think or how to behave mirrors the nation's uncertainty, as well as many citizens' hopelessness, and a newfound vulnerability. The Man of Steel, much like the U.S., had lost his way, which frightened and demoralized many. If something as commanding as a superpower country or a superhero goes into decline, then what are the consequences for both the state and the world? What kind of power vacuum is created and what chaos will result from this new paradigm shift? Would other countries or forces step in and help protect the status quo, or would a new order develop? All of these questions, and many more, filled the minds of real Americans as they watched with trepidation as their country change, seemingly for the worse. Superman was facing a mental and emotional crisis, but a comic book character's psychology paled in comparison with the disturbing things that were happening in the real world. Americans were facing tough times and Superman's struggles provided little reassurance or entertainment for an already overwhelmed nation.

Batman Malaise

As Superman was suffering a mental and emotional collapse, Batman was also beginning to break down but in a very different manner. For several years the Dark Knight had labored in a dark and terrifying world, in which villains became more sinister, and Gotham City was transformed into a jaded and frightening metropolis. Since the late 1960s, the Caped Crusader was fighting against worsening odds and new breeds of madmen who challenged his physical, emotional, and mental resolve. By mid-1978, this constant stress and suffering seemed to take its toll on the Dark Knight, and his adventures assumed a rather dull, plodding turn. The once-electrifying Batman entered a period in which his stories were pedantic and uninspiring. The hero began to resemble a darker, grittier, and more tired version of the corporate family man that Superman embodied during the 1950s and 1960s. Batman's villains continued to be bloodthirsty and their death traps remained dire, but his tales only appeared to be shuffling through the paces, while the Caped Crusader himself looked as if he, too, was trapped in the end of the 1970s doldrums. This lethargy and ready acceptance of the excessively mundane mirrored both the comic book industry and American society as a whole during this period. Comic book publishers in general and DC Comics in particular were experiencing a sales slump due to many factors, including an economic downturn, a shift among readers from print media to television and other forms of entertainment, and rapidly increasing comic book prices caused by inflation and rising base costs. To combat this downward sales trend, and to better compete with Marvel, DC augmented its number of monthly published comic books significantly from 1975 to 1978. Unfortunately, the recession, inflation, and blizzards on the East Coast disrupted sales and forced the company to pare back its titles drastically in late 1978. The publisher's cancellation of a substantial number of its comic book titles has become known as the "DC Implosion." This destruction of much of the company's line serves as a backdrop and a parallel to the unimaginative stories that populate the period's Batman mythology.[12] DC Comics and Batman were both experiencing late-1970s stagnation, but this in turn served as a reflection of life within American society as a whole.

As previously noted, the United States suffered from a host of problems and obstacles during the mid- and late 1970s. Many of these challenges were fueled by reactions to the social and cultural changes of the 1960s. Other difficulties were the result of the societal backlash from the Vietnam War and the Watergate affair, economic problems that included a recession and a mixture of high unemployment and inflation known as stagflation, and the ongoing Cold War with the Soviet Union. All of these ingredients combined to create a bitter and melancholy atmosphere within American society. President Jimmy Carter noted this growing sense of discontent in his famous "Crisis of Confidence Speech" in which the nation's leader noted that the country's citizens had lost faith in the United States and themselves. Carter stated, "The threat is nearly invisible in ordinary ways. It is a crisis of confidence. It is a crisis that strikes at the very heart and soul and spirit of our national will. We can see this crisis in the growing doubt about the meaning of our own lives and in the loss of a unity of purpose for our nation. The erosion of our confidence in the future is threatening to destroy the social and the political fabric of America."[13] The president asserted publicly what many Americans only noted privately or even kept to themselves altogether, namely, a large number of citizens no longer believed in their government or American society in general, and this mistrust was affecting the nation as a whole. A sense of hopelessness and bleakness permeated almost every part of society, and Americans were seemingly caught in a cycle of distrust and apathy. Many people expected life to worsen progressively, and were unsurprised when these beliefs were validated by political or social events that reinforced the country's problems. During this apathetic and angry period, Batman stories began to model society and became uninspired retreads of 1950s and 1960s ideas. Many Americans seemed to be trapped in a downward spiral and Batman, instead of attempting to save them, was content to emulate them.

Two October 1978 Batman-centered comic books are excellent examples of Batman stories that demonstrate American society's growing malaise. The first is *Batman* #304, which contains a seventeen-page main story and an eight-page backup tale. In the primary story, entitled "To Hell with Batman—and Back!" (written by David V. Reed and penciled by John Calnan), a villain named Spook captures, tricks, and tortures the Dark Knight. The narrative begins with a dialogue box that proclaims, "There are no such words as safe or secure in the lexicon of Batman! On every patrol, the invisible twin vultures of death and disaster are overhead... wing-in-wing in grim expectancy biding their time."[14] With these opening words, the writer, Reed, attempts to create a darker and more somber tone, but the story that follows is an unremarkable and unsuccessful effort to fashion a thrilling whodunit text. The story's premise is that Spook has captured and drugged Batman, and now the Dark Knight believes that he has died and returned as a ghost. The tale ends with Batman revealing that he solved the mystery and captured the bad guy, with life returning to normal. The story provides no real mystery because the reader is quickly aware of Spook's ruse and deception, although Batman is not. Since Spook's main purpose is to kill Batman, it is never made clear why the villain does not do this at the beginning of the story and avoid the bizarre deathtrap. While many comic book stories contain convoluted elements and odd plots, this story's lifelessness points up its lack of purpose. This Batman is going through the motions of fighting crime, but lacks purpose and conviction, a statement that is just as true of much of American society as it is of the Dark Knight.

Unlike the first story in *Batman* #304, the issue's backup tale is remarkable in its design and implementation. The eight-page story is "… the first of a dynamite new series of stories based on… the Public Life of Bruce Wayne."[15] In this tale, Bruce Wayne rushes from his tennis game in order to keep an appointment with his personal physician, Douglas Dundee, who was also a friend of Bruce's late father. Dr. Dundee served as a mentor to young Bruce after the murder of Wayne's parents, and Bruce eventually revealed his Batman secret identity to the trusted doctor. In this issue, Dr. Dundee is robbed and forced to carry out a criminal medical treatment during Bruce Wayne's checkup. Bruce quickly disguises himself as the elderly doctor, and, after locating the criminals, thoroughly beats them. The tale ends with Dr. Dundee receiving all the credit and Batman's butler, Alfred, wondering when Bruce Wayne will take time off from his crime-fighting exploits to eat and sleep.[16] This peculiar story was created with the suspect premise that comic book fans would want to read about Bruce Wayne's daily exploits. Added to that already shaky ground is the story development of a billionaire playing tennis, visiting his doctor, failing to prevent a robbery and a crime, and then dressing up as someone else to track down the criminals. These narrative elements are so mundane that it is difficult to understand how, cobbled together, they create a short story. The overall tale suggests that the author was confused and did not understand what to do. In many ways this mirrors 1978 America, a country that had seemingly lost its way and a citizenry that no longer understood how to act. The U.S.'s and Batman's shared crisis was not some titanic external threat, but rather a slowly creeping sense of apathy and disenfranchisement. Only a few years before, the U.S. was unmatched in both its power and its citizens' belief in the nation. Similarly, exciting adventures and death-defying antics previously undergirded Batman and made him a hero to be both respected and embraced. Now both entities had entered a troubling period, and it was unclear what could be done. Batman was floundering, as was the nation around him.

DC Comics also published *Detective Comics* #479 in October 1978 which contains a seventeen-page Batman story and an eight-page Hawkman backup tale. The Batman adventure is the second part of a two-issue storyline in which the Dark Knight battles a new and deadlier version of the villain Clayface. The first bad guy to call himself Clayface was a masked 1940s B-movie actor who had no superpowers at the time of his original appearance. The second Clayface debuted in 1961, and had the ability to change his body into almost any shape imaginable. This new 1978 version of Clayface is Preston Payne, a scientist who injects himself with the 1960s Clayface's blood in an effort to cure a genetic condition. Payne's body soon melts into a claylike appearance and his touch becomes deadly, dissolving anyone with whom he has physical contact. This new Clayface falls in love with a mannequin that he believes is human, and that he imagines enjoys watching him fight for her entertainment. Additionally, Payne feels the need to melt people by touching them, causing him to murder or threaten many of those around him. This third Clayface displays the typical qualities of a late-1970s Batman villain, i.e., he is mentally unstable, deadly and frightening, and has more advanced superpower than his predecessors. This is the same formula that Marty Pasko used in many of his Superman stories of the mid- to late 1970s: enhance a villain like Toyman or Bizarro by changing him from a benign, easily dispersed foe to a horrifying madman. In this Batman storyline, Clayface is psychotic, deadly, and powerful, but he also has no clear-cut objective, and does little that is novel or exciting. In the tale, Batman does not get to be a detective because Clayface has no plan or agenda except wanton destruction. The Dark Knight does not seek a physical fight, because the villain can easily best him. Batman does not go on an adventure, solve a mystery, meet someone exciting, venture into the fantastical, or do a hundred other things that had made stories of the past thrilling and worthwhile. What the Caped Crusader does is chase Clayface, clean up the bad guy's messes, confront the villain, and watch as the madman apparently dies. Batman is no longer a deductive crime fighter who pushes the action forward and works to outsmart and outmaneuver his adversary. Instead, the Dark Knight is reactionary, and waits for Clayface to finally destroy himself with little help from the Caped Crusader.[17] In numerous stories from this period, Batman is neither detective nor superhero, but rather a crime fighter who seems to have lost his way, much like the country that he represented and the readers that followed his monthly adventures.

End of the Decade Fears

As Batman limped towards the end of 1978, Superman was also experiencing the 1970s malaise. As had been the case for numerous years, the Man of Steel was still having difficulty adjusting and readjusting to an ever-changing society. The Metropolis Marvel had fought these changes during the 1960s and early 1970s, but the low sales and the specter of irrelevance forced the Man of Steel to attempt to transform into a superhero with which modern readers could identify. Marvel heroes engaged and appealed to many fans in a way that Superman no longer did. Unfortunately, change did not come easy to the Man of Steel and several attempts had been quickly aborted and were never spoken of again. Superman needed to change while keeping as much of himself as possible. Writers and editors had to figure out what were Superman's core elements that needed to be conserved and what could be stripped away and discarded. The U.S. was also suffering from a similar problem. It was apparent that numerous elements within American society ought to be updated or retired, but few citizens and leaders could agree on what those were and even fewer seemed to possess the fortitude to press for widespread and lasting change. It was in this climate that December 1978 saw the release of *Superman the Movie,* and many filmgoers ended the year accepting the motion picture's tagline, "You'll believe a man can fly!" The movie was popular, and only reinforced the Man of Steel's conservative nature, ironically exacerbating the difficulties he had trying to change for a new generation of comic book readers. Film audiences and the general public accepted the straight-laced and unhip Man of Tomorrow because the Big Blue Boy Scout played well on the big screen. The Man of Steel's heroics were astounding on film, where his old-fashioned nature translated as iconic and timeless. This was not so in comic book stories, where Superman's readership was steadily dropping and many fans who remained were losing interest. The Metropolis Marvel's funny book tales were not iconic, just unexceptional. The hero's successful big-screen exploits and the comic industry's tribulations pushed DC executives to continue to endorse publishing stories centered on a conservative and predictable Man of Steel. Superman was a multimedia product/symbol and not solely a comic book character, and thus his image needed to be protected as such. Superman had always had a difficult time changing, and now many inside and outside of DC did not even want him to. More and more comic book readers disagreed with this assessment, but this seemed to be making less and less of a difference.

The Man of Steel's return to fully embracing his predictable conservative 1950s persona can be seen in multiple stories that were published in 1979. One prime example is *Superman* #335 in which the Man of Tomorrow encounters the fifth-dimension magic imp Mr. Mxyzptlk. In most past stories, Mr. Mxyzptlk had been a merry trickster who pestered the Man of Steel until Superman could convince the creature to say his name backwards and return to his home dimension. This tale followed much the same formula, and begins with Superman and Lois Lane talking about the possibility of getting married. During the conversation, the Man of Steel teases Lois with the idea of matrimony, then declares that it is impossible, because his enemies would fixate on her and this would place her in too much danger. Lois replies, "Oh, come on! That's always been a cop-out—and you know it! I don't have to be married to you to be in danger—just loving you can be risky enough! In the past three years alone, I've been kidnapped seventeen times ... shot at an average of twice a month ... and been the victim of various other kinds of murder-attempts on no less than thirty-eight separate occasions."[18] In this brief passage, writer Marty Pasko not only returns to one of the defining elements of 1950s and 1960s Superman stories, marriage, but also displays how routine and unoriginal the then-current Man of Steel tales remained. Since the 1950s, Lois Lane has generally served two purposes in Superman stories: 1) to advance a plot by getting Superman to marry her, and 2) to advance a plot by being kidnapped, blackmailed, harassed, or having some other type of criminal act intended for her, and thus forcing Superman to rescue her. In this story, as in many others that preceded it, Lois is a passive participant in Superman's world and, although numerous writers have tried to mask this truism, in general Lois has more often than not been used as more of a plot device than a person. While some stories in the early 1970s attempted to transform Ms. Lane into more of a three-dimensional character, this narrative showcases a return to early norms. At the end of this story's first sequence, Superman flies off and intensely ponders how to give Lois superpowers so that she will not be in constant danger. As the young reporter watches the Man of Steel, leave, she ruminates, "He's sweet to want to do that—but *sigh* does he have to do it right this minute?! Oh, well ... like they say: 'strange are the ways of love!'"[19] Although DC published this comic book in 1979, these opening two story pages read like a 1950s romance comic. Superman's writers and editors had seemingly given up on any attempt to modernize the Man of Steel and instead were happy to return to outdated superhero tropes. As American society appeared to be floundering, Superman stories retreated back into a safer and less complicated time.

Superman's romantic problems with Lois Lane were in the first few pages of the comic book, though. Soon Superman has to outwit Mr. Mxyzptlk and send the imp back to his home dimension. Additionally, the Man of Steel must trick Mxyzptlk into returning the hero back to his normal physical state after a super alien creature's bite has transformed Superman into a green scaly beast.[20] The plot and artwork from this issue could have as easily been produced in 1949 as 1979. Another excellent example of Superman returning to his conservative nature and former identity is a Len Wein backup story in November 1979's *Superman* #341. This tale features the return of J. Wilbur Wolfingham, a monocle-sporting, top-hat-wearing con man based on the long-deceased film actor W.C. Fields. Wolfingham first appeared in *Superman* #26 (January/February 1944) and is an unpowered criminal who attempts to con citizens out of their money. The flimflam man was featured in several 1940s and 1950s stories, and fell out of favor by the 1960s, most likely because the overweight, underpowered white-collar criminal is not much of a foe for the Man of Steel. In this issue, Wolfingham attempts to sell a good-luck charm known as a Protecto-Pendant to numerous citizens of Metropolis with the promise that his customers will "... need never know fear again. In moments of mortal peril, the glowing stone in each pendant—part of a certain bauble I chanced upon in the woods one day—will teleport you to safety, as if by magic."[21] Superman tricks the grifter into believing that the pendants actually work and eventually exposes the con man as a cheat and a liar. The story is odd because Superman does a police officer's job and defeats a 1940s-style criminal by using an elaborate ruse. Like the aforementioned Mr. Mxyzptlk tale, this story could easily have been written during the 1940s or 1950s, and indeed it contains many of the elements present in most Superman comic books from that period. As Superman is entering middle age, he seems to be regressing and returning to the more carefree stories and ideas of his youth. Many Americans no longer believed in their nation and Superman apparently no longer believed that he needed to update himself for a modern audience. Superman and his corporate masters seemed satisfied with the Man of Steel embracing his classic self. As change proved more and more difficult, Superman merely stopped trying. For a time, the Man of Steel was willing to accept his overly powerful and conservative identity, and cease the seemingly unrelenting attempts at change.

While Superman was retreating into the safety of his conservative nature, Batman's creators were producing Caped Crusader stories that emphasized not only adventure but also romance, melodrama, and continuing narratives that persisted for months on end. After a brief period of stale stories in the previous months, Batman's tales now featured a number of different plotlines and minor side stories. These soap-opera-type stories were very different from most recent Batman stories, which were usually finished in one or two issues. These long-running storylines forced readers to follow closely several major and minor plot developments over the course of months in order to read the complete story. This meant that each story generally featured Batman, Bruce Wayne, a love interest, several members of Batman's supporting cast, and numerous interconnected plot points, all in one seventeen-page issue. This created an interesting dynamic, in which the Dark Knight's tales at once become both more traditional and more innovative. The idea of action/adventure, romance, and a supporting cast are comic book story staples that creators have relied on since the medium's earliest days. Featuring so many of these core storytelling elements showed that the writers, artists, and editors were returning to superhero basics. These tales also emphasize Batman's extended "family" and interconnect the Caped Crusader with numerous people on whom he depends. This forces the Dark Knight to be less like the early 1970s loner, and more like the 1950s family man who oversaw a large circle of friends and admirers. The length and depth of the storylines showcase innovation and complexity, though. These are highly serialized adventures that create a sophisticated new world that challenges and engages the readers. While Batman remains a crime-fighting superhero, he is now more a part of a larger narrative. The Dark Knight's exploits propel the stories forward, but the supporting cast grounds the hero and forces him to accept a new, more refined role. As the 1970s end, the Caped Crusader's stories are expanding and pressing into new territory. Batman tales were embracing the oxymoronic new traditionalism, in which the Dark Knight's creators updated and redefined core elements. Batman's neotraditionalism mirrors changes that were on the American social horizon. The conservative movement that would soon spawn a Ronald Reagan presidency was gaining steam and Batman, as had continuously been the case, was already prepared to make another important change. Old was new again, and Batman was once more ready to transform for his readers.

Numerous characters stepped to the forefront in 1979 as *Batman* comics embraced a neotraditional structure. The Dark Knight's adventures still contain clichéd villains, overwritten plots, and predictable story twists, but the action moves at a breezy pace while concentrating on several different storylines. This forces the reader to view the Batman stories not as monthly adventures, but as one long-running serialized story with numerous plotlines to follow for a prolonged period of time. Comic book stories have always been interconnected, but this type of storytelling took the idea of narrative unification to a new level while re-embracing classic core comic book concepts like action, adventure, and romance. As Batman battled criminals like Calendar Man, Kite-Man, Firebug, Crazy Quilt, Two-Face, Mr. Freeze, the Gentleman Ghost, and Blockbuster, supporting players demanded a role. Included in most stories are Bruce Wayne's butler, Alfred Pennyworth, and the Gotham City Police Commissioner, James Gordon, two of Batman's most trusted allies. These two longtime Batman associates serve as advisers to Bruce Wayne and the Caped Crusader while showcasing Batman's various roles as billionaire, philanthropist, crime fighter, surrogate law enforcement officer, playboy, etc. No longer is Batman shown just fighting crime; many comic book issues depict Bruce Wayne running his company and jet-setting, while portraying how the costumed hero also liaises with the police. Additionally, in these stories Bruce Wayne attempts to start a relationship with Selina Kyle, the former Catwoman, who is trying to reform and end her criminal ways. Their romance is featured in several issues, and provides a sexual tension that is rarely seen in Batman stories. Selina, the former criminal bad girl, and Bruce Wayne, the straight-laced billionaire with a strange secret and a nearly psychotic need to fight crime. The unlikely pair emphasizes passion and desire over good judgment, which could be seen as a governing principle in Batman's world in general. In a one-page sequence in *Batman* #315 (September 1979), the couple go on a lunch date that has been planned and spoken about in previous issues. The meal ends quickly, though, when Selina throws a glass of water in Bruce's face and storms off, angry that Wayne had asked an employee to investigate the former Catwoman.[22] Later, in eleven panels in *Batman* #318 (December 1979), the couple dances at an exclusive club fashioned onboard a Boeing 747 aircraft. As Bruce courts Selina, the young woman eyes a shipment of priceless artwork, causing the reader to wonder if she actually has reformed.[23] The romance and the possible re-emergence of a popular villain combine to create an unexpected, long-running narrative using traditional core comic book plot elements. This storyline alone could not sustain reader interest for long, but the writer, Len Wein and the editor, Paul Levitz, were betting that readers would enjoy a short one-and-a-half-page insert once a month over the course of several months. The creators were returning Batman to comic book basics, but in a new and inventive way.

One other *Batman* storyline of interest during this period concerned Bruce Wayne's employee Lucius Fox, and his attempt to protect his boss's company. Normally, corporate deal-making and international business mergers would have little place in Batman stories, but this subplot reflects the numerous different types of narratives which were present in *Batman* tales during the end of the 1970s. In his small monthly plot, Lucius Fox attempts to stop a wealthy foreign billionaire named Gregorian Falstaff from harming Wayne Enterprises, the Wayne Foundation in particular, and Gotham City in general. In *Batman* #315, one of Falstaff's employees pursues Lucius and asks for a meeting between the Wayne employee and his boss.[24] During the next several issues Fox considers and accepts the meeting in the hope that he can prevent Falstaff from taking over and destroying Bruce Wayne's company, and receives a job offer from the foreign businessman. Falstaff wishes to hire Fox and use him to ruin Wayne's business interests.

Finally, in *Batman* #318, Fox meets with Falstaff and graciously turns down the billionaire's employment proposal. Falstaff vows to find another way to get what he wants, and sinisterly states that things may not go as pleasantly as they could have, had Fox accepted his offer. This monthly micro-storyline contains little new and nothing revolutionary. Gregorian Falstaff is a character so stereotypical that his presence verges on xenophobia. He is an extremely gluttonous, overweight, corrupt businessman who is constantly eating, and attempting to destroy other companies and much of American society. Falstaff only wants to acquire money and power, and he does not care whom he has to destroy in order to get them. Strangely, Lucius Fox does little to combat Falstaff's plans besides ponder the billionaire's motives, take a meeting, and turn down a job offer.[25] While Falstaff appears later in *Batman* comics published in 1980, Lucius does hardly anything worthwhile for the opening months of the micro-storyline. What is revealing is that this narrative is allowed to build over the course of numerous months, and provides a background plot that eventually becomes the main story in a later issue. While these miniature narratives only show up for a page or two per issue, they are given time to create a coherent and engaging story. This expanded micro-storytelling displays a level of sophistication that was rarely seen in Batman books previously. Though Marvel had been publishing stories like this in some of its comics, Batman had never followed suit. Uniquely, Batman embraced the basic conservative comic book ideas of romance, action, and adventure, but did so in a complex and innovative way. This is a harbinger of the changes that would be coming in the 1980s, as the neotraditional movement transformed the nation by using traditional ideas and narratives viewed and structured in a new way. As the 1970s ended, Batman was not only following cultural and social trends, but was leading the way. The 1980s Reagan era was coming, but that is another story altogether.

Conclusion

During the late 1970s, Superman and Batman once again proved to be reliable indicator superheroes and sometimes bellwether ones as well. From 1976 to 1979, the superpair mirrored American society, and at times both lost their ways. In a post-Watergate, post-Vietnam, and mid-financial and collective crises era, Batman initially became darker and more jaded. The excessively Dark Knight showcased the pain, anger, and terror that many Americans were feeling as they watched their lives become undone. The Caped Crusader continued to battle the forces of evil, but the changing world made him more weary and less hospitable than in years past, adjectives that could also describe the nation as a whole. Towards the latter part of the decade, Batman stories had become simple versions of older tales which bordered on self-parody. By 1979, some stories in *Batman* comics were showing new takes on older narratives, and beginning to display a degree of neotraditionalism that would take hold in American society during the 1980s. Superman, by contrast, chose to continue to embrace his conservative and iconic status as Americans fought bewilderment and fear in the mid- to late 1970s. While the Man of Steel briefly battled enhanced and more deadly villains, this, like many past changes, did not last. By decade's end, Superman was delighted to revert once again to his classic 1950s overly powerful and deeply wholesome self. The Man of Steel's increased assuredness and his return to his mid-century identity spoke to Americans who wanted the world to return to the perceived simple and carefree days of the past. Though these times would never reappear, Superman could serve as a beacon of a different age. Both Batman and Superman ended the 1970s by foreshadowing the coming decade's changes. Batman would become even more famous as the hyperconservative of Frank Miller's *Batman: The Dark Knight Returns*, while Superman would finally be depowered and remade by John Byrne (at least for a while.) As with most other periods, by 1979, Superman and Batman had served their social purposes and were ready to once again reinvent themselves as American society was changing, a task that never ends (much like most everything else in a superhero's career).

Notes

1 Gerry Conway, John Romita, and Carmine Infantino. "The Battle of the Century." *Superman vs. the Amazing Spider-Man* #1 (New York: DC Comics and Marvel Comics, 1976): 51.

2 Conway, et al. *Superman vs.*: 58.

3 Steve Englehart. "Detective Comics (The Batman), 469- 476, Batman: Dark Detective I." *SteveEnglehart.com* Accessed August 16, 2012. http://www.steveenglehart.com/comics/detective%20comics%20469-476.html.

4 Englehart and Marshall Rogers. "The Laughing Fish!" *Detective Comics* #475 (New York: DC Comics, February 1978). Englehart and Rogers. "The Sign of the Joker." *Detective Comics* #476 (New York: DC Comics, March 1978).

5 Michael Eury and Marty Pasko. "Marty Pasko Interview." *The Krypton Companion* (Raleigh, NC: TwoMorrows Publishing, 2007): 157.

6 Marty Pasko and Curt Swan. "The Man Who Played With Death!" *Superman* #305 (New York: DC Comics, November 1976,): 5.

7 Marty Pasko and Curt Swan. "Backwards Battle for the Bizarro World!" *Superman* #306 (New York: DC Comics, December 1976): 17.

8 Gerry Conway and Jose Luis Garcia-Lopez. "Krypton—No More!" *Superman* #307 (New York: DC Comics, January 1977): 1.

9 Conway and Garcia-Lopez. *Superman* #307: 6.

10 Conway and Garcia-Lopez. *Superman* #307: 9.

11 Gerry Conway and Jose Luis Garcia-Lopez. "Blind Hero's Bluff!" *Superman* #309 (New York: DC Comics, March 1977): 17.

12 David R. Black. "The DC Implosion!" Fanzing: The DC Comics Fan Site. Accessed July 2, 2012. http://www.fanzing.com/mag/fanzing27/feature1.shtml. Chris Arrant. "Remembering DC Explosion (and Implosion)." July 21, 2011. iFanboy.com. Accessed July 2, 2012. http://ifanboy.com/articles/remembering-dc-explosion-and-implosion/.

13 Jimmy Carter. "Primary Resources: Crisis of Confidence." July 15, 1979. *American Experience*. Accessed July 5, 2012. http://www.pbs.org/wgbh/americanexperience/features/primary-resources/carter-crisis/.

14 David V. Reed and John Calnan. "To Hell With Batman—and Back!" *Detective Comics* #304 (New York: DC Comics, October 1978): 1.

15 David V. Reed and Win Mortimer. "The Amazing Secret of Dr. Dundee." *Detective Comics* #304 (New York: DC Comics, October 1978): 19.

16 Reed and Mortimer. *Detective*: 17-25.

17 Len Wein and Marshall Rogers. "If a Man Be Made of Clay!" *Detective Comics* #479 (New York: DC Comics, September/October 1978).

18 Marty Pasko and Curt Swan. "Mxyzptlk Spelled Backward Is T-R-O-U-B-L-E." *Superman* #335 (New York: DC Comics, May 1979): 3.

19 Pasko and Swan. *Superman* #335: 3.

20 Pasko and Swan. *Superman* #335: 9-17.

21 Len Wein and Curt Swan. "The Man Who Could Cancel Catastrophe!" *Superman* #341 (New York: DC Comics, November 1979): 13.

22 Len Wein and Irv Novick. "Danger in the Wing!" *Batman* #315 (New York, DC Comics, September 1979): 8.

23 Len Wein and Irv Novick. "My City Burns at Both Ends—It Will Not Last the Night!" *Batman* #318 (New York: DC Comics, December 1979): 5-6.

24 Wein and Novick. *Batman* #315: 4-5.

25 Wein and Novick. *Batman* #318: 9-10.

In an often discussed scene in the 2004 Quentin Tarantino film *Kill Bill 2*, David Carradine's title character, Bill, gives an impassioned speech about Superman. Bill attempts to explain his actions during the two *Kill Bill* films by using the Man of Steel as a metaphor. He soliloquizes:

> As you know, I'm quite keen on comic books, especially the ones about superheroes. I find the whole mythology surrounding superheroes fascinating. Take my favorite superhero, Superman. Not a great comic book. Not particularly well drawn. But the mythology... The mythology is not only great, it's unique... Now, a staple of the superhero mythology is, there's the superhero and there's the alter ego. Batman is actually Bruce Wayne, Spider-Man is actually Peter Parker. When that character wakes up in the morning, he's Peter Parker. He has to put on a costume to become Spider-Man and it is in that characteristic Superman stands alone. Superman didn't become Superman; Superman was born Superman. When Superman wakes up in the morning, he's Superman; his alter ego is Clark Kent. His outfit with the big red "S"– that's the blanket he was wrapped in as a baby when the Kents found him. Those are his clothes. What Kent wears– the glasses, the business suit–that's the costume. That's the costume Superman wears to blend in with us. Clark Kent is how Superman views us. And what are the characteristics of Clark Kent? He's weak... He's unsure of himself... He's a coward. Clark Kent is Superman's critique on the whole human race.[1]

Fig. 0.6
Batman in the 1970s.

Many comic book fans have argued extensively about the validity of Carradine's speech (as they are wont to do), but in reality, the most consequential thing about the scene is that it displays Superman's and Batman's flexible roles in American culture. People can and will debate the heroes' true natures because neither really has a genuine self. The characters' backgrounds and personalities are an amalgam of highlighted plot elements and shifting story types produced by numerous authors since the late 1930s. The Man of Steel and the

Dark Knight change, adapt, transform, adjust, revise, and recreate themselves again and again to such an extent that it is impossible to assert what defines the "true" Superman or Batman. The heroes have no "true" selves because they are works in progress that must always be prepared to adjust to new times and different social needs. The superpair take on the roles that Americans demand, and if they do not, then they risk becoming outdated and archaic and eventually will only exist as a distant memory of a world that used to be. There is no "real" Superman or Batman because they were created to become what we need when we need it, and when they no longer fulfill their purpose they will disappear.

American culture is littered with faint remembrances of characters who flourished for a season and then became inconsequential and vanished. The Yellow Kid was once a national phenomenon and now only historians and old comic strip fans remember the political cartoon character. Captain Marvel's adventures outsold Superman's during comic books' early days, but now the Big Red Cheese is a second-string character barely known to most Americans. These once-popular characters, and hundreds of others, were unable to transition as the U.S. changed, and thus were left behind as the country moved forward. Superman and Batman have become part of a uniquely American mythology because they were able to transform as needed while creating the illusion that they were remaining the same. David Carradine's character in *Kill Bill* is both right and wrong about Superman's and Batman's identities, because in reality the two have no real selves. Think about Superman for a moment, what are his key traits? He can fly? In his earliest adventures he could not. He is the lone survivor of a doomed planet? In many stories there is an entire planet of Kryptonians that continue to exist. He fights for "truth, justice, and the American way?" Actually he has changed so many times over the years that it is difficult to say what the Man of Steel fights for and the "American way" sound bite comes from the Superman radio and television shows. Batman is even more difficult to define, because he has transformed much more than Superman since his inception. Neither superhero can be fully explained from their beginnings until the present day with a quick and easy analysis. The pair has changed too much and too often for such a treatment. Much like Americans and their society, the superhero founding fathers' pasts are messy, often unpleasant, and generally difficult to understand. Also, like many Americans, Superman and Batman focus largely on the present and strive to be the heroes that current American society needs, without extensive baggage from bygone days. The two heroes have survived, and often thrived, for over seventy years because they are important to current Americans and speak to modern social problems and contemporary cultural necessities. The Man of Steel and the Dark Knight have changed often because they have needed to and because Americans have demanded it.

Notes

1 *Kill Bill 2*. Quentin Tarantino, director. Miramax Films, 2004.

BIBLIOGRAPHY

"1960 Comic Book Sales Figures." *The Comics Chronicles.* Accessed May 17, 2012. http://www.comichron.com/yearlycomicssales/1960s/1960.html.

"1965 Comic Book Sales Figures." *The Comics Chronicles.* Accessed May 17, 2012. http://www.comichron.com/yearlycomicssales/1960s/1965.html.

"1966 Comic Book Sales Figures." *The Comics Chronicles.* Accessed May 17, 2012. http://www.comichron.com/yearlycomicssales/1960s/1966.html.

"1969 Comic Book Sales Figures." *The Comics Chronicles.* Accessed June 17, 2012. http://www.comichron.com/yearlycomicssales/1960s/1969.html.

Adams, Neal. Cover image. *Superman's Girl Friend Lois Lane* #80. New York: DC Comics, January 1968.

Adams. Cover image. *Superman's Girl Friend Lois Lane* #85. New York: DC Comics, August 1968.

Arrant, Chris. "Remembering DC Explosion (and Implosion)." July 21, 2011. *iFanboy.com.* Accessed July 2, 2012. http://ifanboy.com/articles/remembering-dc-explosion-andimplosion/.

Beck, C.C. "Captain Marvel and the Atomic War." *DC's Greatest Imaginary Stories.* New York: DC Comics, 2005.

Bates, Cary, and Nick Cardy. "Mystery Mission to Metropolis." *Superman* #281. New York: DC Comics, November 1974.

Bates and Bob Oksner. "The Ten Deadly Visions of the 100." *Superman's Girl Friend Lois Lane* #123. New York: DC Comics, June 1972.

Berra, Yogi. "Yogi Berra Quotes." *Yogi-isms.* Accessed on June 12, 2012. http://www.umpirebob.com/DATA/yogiisms.htm.

Black, David R. "The DC Implosion!" Fanzing: The DC Comics Fan Site. Accessed July 2, 2012. http://www.fanzing.com/mag/fanzing27/feature1.shtml.

Broome, John. "Mystery of the Menacing Mask." *Detective Comics* #327. New York: DC Comics, May 1964.

Cameron, Don, and Jack Burnley. "The Boy Who Wanted to Be Robin!" Batman #15 in *Batman: The Dark Knight Archives.*

Cameron and Burnley. "Swastika Over the White House!" *Batman* #14 in *Batman: The Dark Knight Archives.* New York: DC Comics, 2003.

Cameron and Burnley. "The Two Futures!" *Batman* #15 in *Batman: The Dark Knight Archives.*

Carter, Jimmy. "Primary Resources: Crisis of Confidence." July 15, 1979. *American Experience.* Accessed July 5, 2012. http://www.pbs.org/wgbh/americanexperience/features/primary-resources/carter-crisis/.

Coleman, Jerry, and Bernard Bailey. "Bat-Mite Meets Mr. Mxyzptlk." *World's Finest Comics* #113. New York: DC Comics, November 1960.

Conway, Gerry, John Romita, and Carmine Infantino. "The Battle of the Century." *Superman vs. The Amazing Spider-Man* #1. New York: DC Comics and Marvel Comics, 1976.

Conway and Jose Luis Garcia-Lopez. "Blind Hero's Bluff!" *Superman* #309. New York: DC Comics, March 1977.

Conway and Garcia-Lopez. "Krypton–No More!" *Superman* #307. New York: DC Comics, January 1977.

Cronin, Brian. "Comic Book Urban Legends Revealed #49!" May 4, 2006. *Comic Book Resources.* Accessed March 8, 2012. http://goodcomics.comicbookresources.com/2006/05/04/comic-book-urban-legends-revealed-49/.

Daniels, Les. *Batman: The Complete History*. San Francisco, CA: Chronicle Books, 2004.

Daniels. *Superman: The Complete History*. San Francisco, CA: Chronicle Books, 1998.

Englehart, Steve. "Detective Comics (The Batman), 469-476, Batman: Dark Detective I." *SteveEnglehart.com*. Accessed August 16, 2012. http://www.steveenglehart.com/comics/detective%20comics%20469-476.html.

Englehart and Marshall Rogers. "The Laughing Fish!" *Detective Comics* #475. New York: DC Comics, February 1978.

Englehart and Rogers. "The Sign of the Joker." *Detective Comics* #476. New York: DC Comics, March 1978.

Eury, Michael, and Marty Pasko. "Marty Pasko Interview." *The Krypton Companion*. Raleigh, NC: TwoMorrows Publishing, 2007.

"The Evolution of Batman." June 21, 2007. *AMC Blog*. Accessed June 18, 2012. http://blogs.amctv.com/movie-blog/2007/06/the-evolution-o.php.

Finger, Bill, and Bob Kane. "The Case of the Chemical Syndicate." *Detective Comics* #27 in *The Batman Chronicles, Volume 1*. New York: DC Comics, 2005.

Finger and Kane. "The Case of the Prophetic Pictures." *Detective Comics* #42 in *Batman Archives, Volume 1*. New York: DC Comics, 1997.

Finger and Kane. "The Horde of the Green Dragon." *Detective Comics* #39 in *Batman Archives, Volume 1*. New York: DC Comics, 1997.

Finger and Kane. "Introducing Robin, the Boy Wonder." *Detective Comics* #38 in *The Batman Chronicles, Volume 1*. New York: DC Comics, 2005.

Finger and Kane. "The Land Behind the Light." *Detective Comics* #44 in *Batman Archives, Volume 1*. New York: DC Comics, 1997.

Finger and Kane. "The Spies." *Detective Comics* #37 in *The Batman Chronicles, Volume 1*. New York: DC Comics, 2005.

Finger and Sheldon Moldoff. "Robin Dies at Dawn." *Batman* #156. New York: DC Comics, June 1963.

Finger and Charles Paris. "The New Crimes of Two-Face." *Batman* #68. New York: DC Comics, December 1951.

Finger and Leonard Star. "The Origin of the Bat-Cave." *Detective Comics* #204. New York: DC Comics, March 1954.

Fleisher, Michael L. *The Great Superman Book*. New York: Warner Books, 1978.

Fox, Gardner, and Carmine Infantino. "Inside Story of the Outsider." *Detective Comics* #356. New York: DC Comics, October 1966.

Fox and Infantino. "The Million Dollar Debut on Batgirl!" *Detective Comics* #359 *in Showcase Presents: Batgirl, Volume 1*. New York: DC Comics, 2007.

Fox and Infantino. "Remarkable Ruse of the Riddler." *Batman* #171. New York: DC Comics, May 1965.

Fox and Infantino. "The True False-Face of Batman." *Detective Comics* #363 in *Showcase Presents: Batgirl, Volume 1*. New York: DC Comics, 2007.

Grandinetti, Fred. "Remembering Kathy Kane: The First Batwoman." *Newsarama*. Accessed June 27, 2012. http://web.archive.org/web/20070929132840/http://www.newsarama.com/dcnew/Batwoman/BatwomanHistory.htm.

Hadju, David. *The Ten-Cent Plague: The Great Comic Book Scare and How It Changed America*. New York: Picador, 2009.

Haney, Bob, and Neal Adams. "And Hellgrammite Is His Name." *The Brave and the Bold* #80 in *Batman Illustrated by Neal Adams*. New York: DC Comics, 2003.

Haney and Adams. "The Track of the Hook." *The Brave and the Bold* #79 in *Batman Illustrated By Neal Adams*. New York: DC Comics, 2003.

Jones, Gerald. *Men of Tomorrow: Geeks, Gangsters, and the Birth of the Comic Book*. New York: Basic Books, 2004.

Kanigher, Robert, and Curt Swan. "I Am Curious (Black)!" *Superman's Girl Friend Lois Lane* #106. New York: DC Comics, November 1970.

Kennedy, John F. Inaugural Address. January 20, 1961. *The American Presidency Project*. Accessed May 12, 2012. http://www.presidency.ucsb.edu/ws/index.php?pid=8032.

Kirby, Jack. "A Bug Thing in a Deep Scottish Lake." *Superman's Pal Jimmy Olsen* #144. New York: DC Comics, December 1971.

Lee, Stan and Sol Brodsky. "The Origin of Stuporman!" *Not Brand Echh* #7. New York, Marvel Comics, April 1967.

Letter Column. *Superman's Girl Friend Lois Lane* #125. New York: DC Comics, August 1972.

Levick, Diane. "The 'Liberation' of Lois Lane." *The Michigan Daily*. July 29, 1972. *Google News*. Accessed August 21, 2012. http://news.google.com/

Maggin, Elliot S! and Curt Swan. "Must There Be A Superman?" *Superman* #247 in *The Greatest Superman Stories Ever Told*. New York: DC Comics, 1987.

Maggin. "Must There Be A Superman?" *Superman Through the Ages*. Accessed July 27, 2012. http://supermanthrutheages.com/esm/must.php.

McKay, Holly. "Superman Renounces His U.S. Citizenship in 900th Issue of Action Comics." Foxnews.com. Accessed December 20, 2011. http://www.foxnews.com/entertainment/2011/04/28/superman-renounces-citizenship-900th-issue/.

Mockridge, Norton. "This Wonderful World." *Reading Eagle*. May 4, 1970. *Google News*. Accessed June 17, 2012. http://news.google.com/newspapers?nid=1955&dat=19700504&id=Uy-IrAAAAIBAJ&sjid=2J8FAAAAIBAJ&pg=1889,2792702.

Niven, Larry. "Man of Steel, Woman of Kleenex." Accessed on June 19, 2012. http://www.rawbw.com/~svw/superman.html# Reprinted.

O'Neil, Dennis, and Neal Adams. "Daughter of the Demon." *Batman* #232. New York: DC Comics, June 1971.

O'Neil and Adams. "The Joker's Five-Way Revenge." *Batman* #251. New York: DC Comics, September 1973.

O'Neil and Adams. "The Secret of the Waiting Graves." *Detective Comics* #395. New York: DC Comics, January 1970.

O'Neil and Ed Gross. "Exclusive Interview: Denny O'Neil on Humanizing Superman." January 26, 2009. *ComicBookMovie.com*. Accessed on May 24, 2012. http://www.comicbookmovie.com/fansites/VoicesFromKrypton/news/?a=6067.

O'Neil and Irv Novick. "Catwoman's Circus Caper!" *Batman* #256. New York: DC Comics, October 1974.

O'Neil and Curt Swan. "Superman Breaks Loose." *Superman* #233 in *DC Comics Classics Library, Superman: Kryptonite Nevermore*. New York: DC Comics, 2009.

Pasko, Marty, and Curt Swan. "Backwards Battle for the Bizarro World!" *Superman* #306. New York: DC Comics, December 1976.

Pasko and Swan. "The Man Who Played With Death!" *Superman* #305. New York: DC Comics, November 1976.

Pasko and Swan. "Mxyzptlk Spelled Backward Is T-R-O-U-B-L-E." *Superman* #335. New York: DC Comics, May 1979.

Reed, David V., and John Calnan. "To Hell With Batman—and Back!" *Detective Comics* #304. New York: DC Comics, October 1978.

Reed and Win Mortimer. "The Amazing Secret of Dr. Dundee." *Detective Comics* #304. New York: DC Comics, October 1978.

Robbins, Frank, and Neal Adams. "Challenge of the Man-Bat." *Detective Comics* #400. New York: DC Comics, June 1970.

"Secret Origins of the Batman TV Show, Part One! Batman Begins." *Dial B for Blog*. Accessed May 18, 2012. http://www.dialbforblog.com/archives/204/.

Siegel, Jerry, and Joe Shuster. "America's Secret Weapon." *Superman* #23 in *Superman: From the Thirties to the Seventies*. New York: Crown Publishers, Inc., 1971.

Siegel and Shuster. "The Economic Enemy." *Superman* # 4 in *The Superman Chronicles, Volume 3*. New York: DC Comics, 2007.

Siegel and Shuster. "How Superman Would End the War." *Look* Magazine. February 27, 1940. Superman Through the Ages. Accessed July 2, 2012. http://superman.nu/tales2/endsthewar/.

Siegel and Shuster. "Revolution in San Monte." *Action Comics* #2 in *The Superman Chronicles, Volume 1*. New York: DC Comics, 2006.

Siegel and Shuster. "The Slot Machine Racket." *Superman* #5 in *The Superman Chronicles, Volume 3*. New York: DC Comics, 2007.

Siegel and Shuster. "Superman in the Slums." *Action Comics* #8 in *The Superman Chronicles, Volume 1*. New York: DC Comics, 2006.

Siegel and Shuster. "Superman's Super-Campaign." Action Comics #18 in *The Superman Chronicles*, Volume 2. New York: DC Comics, 2007.

Siegel and Shuster. "Superman vs. the Cab Protective League." *Action Comics* #13 in *The Superman Chronicles, Volume 1*. New York: DC Comics, 2006.

Siegel and Shuster. "Wanted Superman." *Action Comics* #9 in *The Superman Chronicles, Volume 1*. New York: DC Comics, 2006.

Wein, Len, and Neal Adams. "Moon of the Wolf." *Batman* #255. New York: DC Comics, March 1974.

Wein and Irv Novick. "Danger in the Wing!" *Batman* #315. New York: DC Comics, September 1979.

Wein and Novick. "My City Burns at Both Ends—It Will Not Last the Night!" *Batman* #318. New York: DC Comics, December 1979.

Wein and Marshall Rogers. "If a Man Be Made of Clay!" Detective Comics #479. New York: DC Comics, September/October 1978.

Wein and Curt Swan. "The Man Who Could Cancel Catastrophe!" *Superman* #341. New York: DC Comics, November 1979.

Wheeler, Andrew. "The Gayness of Batman: A Brief History [Opinion]." April 30, 2012. *Comics Alliance.* Accessed May 12, 2012. http://www.comicsalliance.com/2012/04/30/the-gayness-of-batman-a-brief-history-opinion-morrison/.

Wright, Bradford W. *Comic Book Nation: The Transformation of Youth Culture in America.* Baltimore: Johns Hopkins University Press, 2001.

INDEX

Note:
Page numbers in italics indicate illustrations; an asterisk (*) indicates a comic book character.

COLOPHON

Molly Q. Cort
Editor

Bruce Ian Meader
Designer

Lisa Mauro
Production

RIT Print & Postal Hub
Printing

Adobe Caslon Pro, Neutraface 2
Typefaces

Color Xpressions Elite
Text and Cover Paper